H
'N

Published by
EMI Music Archives
1-3 Uxbridge Road
Hayes, Middlesex
UB4 0SY

ISBN 0 9509293 1 X

First Published 1984

COPYRIGHT.

Barraud, 92, Bold Str Liverpool
and at 263, Oxford Street, London. N

A photograph of the Original Nipper

CONTENTS

Prelude

'Nipper' the famous 'His Master's Voice' Dog was born one hundred years ago this year. To celebrate this event EMI Music Archives is publishing this 'Guide To Collecting Nipper Souvenirs'.

The reader will note references to 'Nipperie'. 'Nipperie' is the name that, years ago, one of the authors and his colleagues gave to the pieces of 'Nipper' ephemera that were then fairly commonplace in second hand junk shops, market stalls and jumble sales.

Alas, no longer are any of the 707 articles illustrated in this volume so easily found and cheaply acquired.

Collectors who already have these 'Nipper' souvenirs tenaciously hold on to their discoveries. The problem of supply has been greatly exacerbated in recent years during which extensive redevelopment has almost eliminated the small old fashioned record shops in which so many desirable pieces of 'Nipperie' were disposed. A few years ago, as these old shops were being demolished or modernized, many a handsome glass pelmet or H.M.V. Clock were to be obtained by a few pound notes judiciously placed into the dusty hands of the foreman of the demolition gang. Today, however, these chances occur less frequently and the collector is drawn more and more into the expensive Antique and Collector's shops as the main source of supply of these delectables.

The authors think that this is the first attempt to gather together a large body of information on the material available to the collector of 'Nipperie'. In compiling this Guide they have not attempted to produce a complete listing, indeed the limitations of space have prevented the inclusion of every known variation within each broad section. However, an effort has been made to include at least a few examples of each genre known to the authors and to illustrate as many of these as possible.

Gathering together this information was by no means the simple task it might at first appear. The Companies seem not to have retained any systematic listing, or indeed any listing at all, of 'Nipper' souvenirs and advertising that they have issued through the years. Presumably this material was treated as pure ephemera and when it had run its course the background paperwork was destroyed. Thus it is that many desirable pieces of 'Nipperie' remain unknown until a lucky find by a collector uncovers them.

We have tried to avoid generalizations and assumptions and to include only items we have actually seen or found publicity for. However, we must admit that there are instances when, despite our best intentions, it has been necessary to make a stab at a date or two.

Readers owning pieces of 'Nipperie' not mentioned within these pages are invited to write to Mrs. Ruth Edge, Archivist, EMI Music Archives, 1-3 Uxbridge Road, Hayes, Middlesex UB4 0SY, sending a full description or preferably a photograph of the item(s). This information will be gratefully acknowledged and filed for future reference should the opportunity arise to issue a revised and enlarged edition of this Guide.

The Right to the 'His Master's Voice' Trademark on records, gramophones etc., is held by different Groups for various parts of the world. Basically these are EMI (Electric & Musical Industries Ltd); J.V.C. (Japanese Victor Company) and RCA (Radio Corporation of America). All of these companies, or their subsidiaries, have produced 'Nipper' material of interest to the collector.

The authors feel that many collectors who may have a consuming interest in the 'Nipper' souvenirs themselves could well have little or no desire to become entangled in the sometimes complex corporate threads which bind the various companies together. They have, therefore, kept the corporate aspect as simple as possible within the main body of the text. Many companies changed their titles over the years, for simplicity, and to show the controlling interest at the time, when mentioning the French, German, Italian and Spanish Companies within the EMI Group, we have described these as 'The Gramophone Company's French Branch' etc.

Readers wishing to learn more of these corporate relationships will find brief key information included in the 'Nipper Chronology' at the end of this volume.

One further word, your collection of Records, Gramophones and pieces of 'Nipperie' grows more valuable as the years pass. Take every precaution to protect these valuables against vandals and burglars. As The Gramophone Company warned in its House Magazine 'The Voice' for February 1935:

Cat burglars shin up water pipes
And risk a prison fate
By pinching silly things like pearls
And gold and silver plate.

Dog burglars have a bit more sense
And show a pretty choice
By chancing it for something good—
They take 'His Master's Voice.'

The Original Painting of 'His Master's Voice' and the Mystery of the Missing Official Replicas

There can be little doubt that the topmost pinnacle of achievement for a collector of 'Nipperie' must be the possession of one of the original Barraud copies of his famous 'His Master's Voice' painting. Failing this, at a slightly lower level, would be the acquisition of one of the official copies made by other artists. This possibly is not as remote or absurd as it first might appear, and, what is more, we are not suggesting an act of burglary at the office of EMI Music to achieve it!

The full story of how the original painting came to be made and how the Company acquired it is told in 'The Story of Nipper and the His Master's Voice Picture' written by Leonard Petts with an introduction by Frank Andrews. This is published by Ernie Bayly, The Talking Machine Review, 19 Glendale Road, Bournemouth — price £2 + postage (illus no. 4). The reader is referred to this publication for additional information.

Over the years a considerable number of copies of Francis Barraud's painting 'His Master's Voice' have been produced. A brief summary listing the replicas of the painting made by the original artist and the known authorized copies by other painters is given below:

OFFICIAL COPIES KNOWN TO HAVE BEEN MADE OF THE 'HIS MASTER'S VOICE' PAINTING

Paintings by Francis Barraud

Apart from the original, (36 inches × 28 inches), probably painted during the Autumn of 1898-January 1899, Francis Barraud is known to have produced twenty-four replicas during the years 1913-1924. Thus, twenty-five Barraud paintings were officially commissioned by The Gramophone Company.

The original painting naturally stayed with The Gramophone Company in England. Of the twenty-four replicas, it is known that one went to E.R. Johnson, President of the Victor Company in Camden U.S.A., one was sent to Victor for onward transmission to Emile Berliner in Montreal and three copies, including two which were slightly smaller than the original, being 27 inches × 21 inches, for Messrs Atkinson, Staats and Middleton, Directors of the Victor Company. Twelve further copies were commissioned from Barraud for the Victor Company on April 11th 1922. These were for the Company to present certain of their clients with 'authentic copies'.

The Victor Company therefore received seventeen Barraud copies, including the copy sent on to Montreal, the remaining seven, plus the Original, going to the British Company. The latter group included one which the artist made as a gift for the Company (1st February 1923) and which is known as the 'Chinese

1

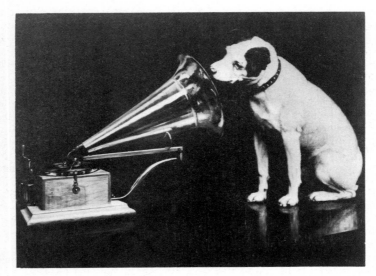

2

Copy'. This is an exact copy of the original, the phonograph being painted in and then over-painted with the famous Trademark gramophone. There are notes on the backs of the paintings to show which is the original and which the Chinese copy.

In addition to the full sized replicas there was a miniature copy in oils which Barraud painted as a personal gift for Alfred Clark (Managing Director of the Gramophone Company).

In the Spring of 1900 Francis Barraud painted a small watercolour (12 inches × 10 inches) of 'His Master's Voice'. This picture was exhibited during March 1900 at the Royal Institute of Painters and Watercolourists where it was sold for 15 Guineas (£15.75). An interesting footnote may be added here. On April 20th 1956, the Executor of an estate wrote to the Company offering the watercolour for sale. It was purchased by the Company.

Since Barry Owen (Managing Director of The Gramophone Company Ltd) had expressed a special interest in the watercolour, Barraud agreed to paint another copy for Owen's personal use. This was painted in exactly the same style as the one exhibited. Barry Owen purchased this and it is believed that he took it with him to the U.S.A. when he left the Company in March 1906.

Towards the end of Francis Barraud's life and after his death in 1924, several other artists were called on to make replicas:

Christian Jacobson
The Danish painter Christian Jacobson was commissioned to make two copies for the Scandinavian Branches. The backs of these paintings indicate that the copies were made in 1923, one year *before* the death of Francis Barraud.

Edmond Dyer
A memo to Alfred Clark, dated April 8th 1924, indicates that the artist Edmond Dyer 'who does a considerable amount of copying for the British Museum' was producing copies of the 'His Master's Voice' picture. It seems that these copies, the number and measurements of which is untraced, were for the Victor Company in Camden U.S.A. and despatch was promised for the following week. Nothing more is known of these.

H.M. Paget
H.M. Paget made the next copy in February 1925.

C.H. Thompson
During September 1926, Mr C.H. Thompson of St. Buryan in Cornwall, painted two replicas. Two more from his brush followed in February 1927, one in February 1928, one in October 1928, two in August 1929, and a final 4 in 1930 — a total of twelve in all which were full sized replicas. In December 1935 he painted twelve small pictures which The Gramophone Company intended for distribution to Electric Supply Monopolies.

An Unkown Dutch Artist
Two replicas were made by an unkown Dutch artist. The paintings are unsigned and undated; however it is known that they were with the Company's Dutch Branch in 1928 and so were probably made during the mid 1920's.

Unofficial Copies
It is known that a copy was made by JULIAN BARROW, an employee of William Drown and Sons, whilst one of the Barraud copies was there for cleaning.

As recently as the Spring of 1978 another copyist WILLIAM GREEN, who worked as a warehouseman at Harrison's Hayes Mill produced a fine copy of the 'His Master's Voice' painting. The result, framed in an antique gold frame (illus no. 3) was such a success that EMI held a special press conference at which William's copy was displayed next door to Barraud's original.

In 1928 all traced replicas painted by Francis Barraud which had been sent to overseas branches were recalled to Head Office and exchanged for copies by other artists. This, of course, did not involve those sent to the Victor Company in America.

Thus, there should be the Original and at least forty-three full sized or near to full sized copies of the 'His Master's Voice' painting, plus a further unknown number of Dyer copies, somewhere around the world.

Strangely, only a handful of these can now be positively accounted for. The present situation of all copies that can now be traced is given below:

KNOWN PRESENT LOCATION OF ALL TRACED COPIES

Barraud (produced Original + 24 copies)

The Original	This is now in the Office of Bhaskar Menon, Chairman and Chief Executive of EMI Music at 30 Gloucester Place, London W1.
The Chinese Copy	With Capitol Records Inc., Capitol Tower, Hollywood, U.S.A.
A 1919 Copy	This is now in the Board Room at 20 Manchester Square, London W1.
A 1920 Copy	This is at the office of EMI Music Ltd., 30 Gloucester Place, London W1.
a second 1920 Copy	This is also at 30, Gloucester Place.
Copy of unknown date	This was presented by the Company to the Hayes Local History Association and is held at the Hayes Public Library.
Copy of unknown date	It is thought that this was destroyed in the disastrous fire at the H.M.V. Oxford Street Store on Boxing Day 1937.
Exhibition Watercolour	This is believed to be in the possession of a retired senior member of the Company's staff.

Christian Jacobson (produced two copies)

Copy of 1923	With the Swedish Company in Stockholm
Copy of 1923	With the Danish Company in Copenhagen

H.M. Paget (produced one copy)

Copy of 1925	With the Electrola Company in Cologne

Edmund Dyer (unknown number of copies)
No copies traced

C.H. Thompson (produced twelve full sized and twelve miniature copies)
Copy of June-July 1929   This is with the Italian Company in Milan
Copy of unknown date   Now in 'The Dog and Trumpet' public house in Marlborough Street, London.
One miniature   With the Managing Director of EMI Music Publishing, Charing Cross Road, London.

Unknown Dutch Artist (produced two copies)
Two undated copies   These are both at Heemstede in Holland with the Dutch Company.

Julian Barrow (produced one copy)
Undated copy   This is in the entrance hall of EMI's Abbey Road Recordng Studios in St. John's Wood, London.

William Green (produced one copy)
Copy of 1978   This is in the personal possession of the artist.

We now come to the point of special interest to the collector. If we take away the totals of the second table from those given in the first, we find an alarming number of these official copies of 'His Master's Voice' paintings to be unaccounted for.

Incredibly there are at least eighteen Francis Barraud full sized copies, plus two miniatures that can not now be firmly accounted for. Knowledge of the present whereabouts of Thompson copies is even more sparse. Ten full sized and eleven miniatures having disappeared. In addition, there is the whole of the 'Nipper' output of Dyer which seems to have vanished without trace.

The last known position of these now 'missing' paintings is detailed below:

THE MISSING PAINTINGS

Francis Barraud
1 full sized copy
(unkown date)
Last known to be in
England

There is a note in the Archive files that this picture was transferred to Morphy Richards (then a Company within the EMI Group) in 1961. When asked about it some years ago Morphy Richards stated that they did not know where it was. The matter was not pursued and this painting must, therefore, be considered mislaid, if not completely lost.

16 full sized copies
Known to have been
sent to the U.S.A.

It is not known to the authors where any of the Barraud copies originally sent to the States now are. Mr Mort Gaffin of RCA tells us that the Company do have two copies of the painting in their New York

3

The story of 'Nipper' and the 'His Master's Voice' picture painted by Francis Barraud

4

offices, however, he does not think they are by Barraud. One of the authors has seen the copy hanging in the suite of the President of RCA at Rockerfeller Centre. He thought that this did not have the stamp of a Barraud and wondered whether it might have been one of the Dyer copies.

1 full sized copy
Last known to be
in Montreal

A request to the Canadian Company for information of this copy produced no reply.

1 miniature (in oils)
Last known to be
in Britain

This is the copy made for Alfred Clark. It is not known what happened to this or even if it was still in his possession at the time of his death in 1950.

1 miniature (in
watercolour)
Last though to be
in the U.S.A.

This is the copy made for Barry Owen. It is thought that he took it with him when he returned to the States in 1906. It has now been lost sight of.

C.H. Thompson
4 full sized copies of
unknown date
Last known to be
in France

These are thought to have been *destroyed* in France during the 1939-45 War. However, their actual destruction has not been confirmed.

1 full sized copy
(unknown date)
Last known to be
in France

This was said to be with the French Company in 1961. France informs us that they do still have a painting *but they do not think it is by Thompson.*

1 full sized copy
Last known to be
in Australia

An undated list in the Archive states that this was sent to Messrs Hoffnung (then the Company's Australian Agent). The Australian Company informs us that they still have a copy of the painting *but it is not thought to be a Thompson.*

Although both France and Australia doubt that their copies of the painting are by Thompson, the question is, if they were not, who are they by? There are no other copies by other painters that are known to have been in the possession of The Gramophone Company and so available for transmission to its Branch Companies, which have not been accounted for. The matter remains unsolved and must await further inspection of the paintings.

4 full sized copies

An undated list in the Archives states that these were last known to be in:
1 copy in Budapest
1 copy in Prague
1 copy in Alexandria
1 copy in Britain
All have now been lost sight of.

11 miniature copies
(in oils)

These are the paintings The Gramophone Company is said to have presented to various 'Electrical Supply Monopolies'. We have no list of the original recipients nor do we know the present situation of any of these eleven miniatures.

Edmund Dyer
Size and number of   All trace of these paintings has now been lost.
paintings is unknown
Last thought to have
been shipped to the
U.S.A.

We do not suggest that all of these 'lost' paintings are just lying around waiting to be picked up by eager 'Nipper' collectors. It seems almost certain that a number of the Barraud American copies will turn up in some odd corner of the R.C.A. organization. However, there does seem to be a good chance that at least some of them will be tucked away in some dusty attic or remain unrecognised and untreasured in some antique or junk shop around the world. Nipper collectors everywhere, 'gird up your loins' and search out this hidden golden treasure trove!

Remember, there are eighteen full (or near full) sized Barraud copies and two Barraud miniatures still at large. In addition, ten full sized and eleven miniature copies by Thompson and the whole of the Dyer output also to be rediscovered.

If you succeed in finding and acquiring one of these you will certainly have scored a triumph over all your collector friends!

Reproductions of
the Painting

Barraud's original painting was delivered to The Gramophone Company's offices on October 17th 1899 and with it the Company received the sole right of 'Reproducing the picture on trade circulars, on catalogues and heading of notepaper'.

Immediately plans were made to produce fine reproductions of the painting and negotiations for the purchase of the copyright of the picture began, although the actual transfer of the copyright was not completed until January 1st 1900.

By December 5th 1899 proofs of the first reproductions of the picture were available (printed by Rembrandt & Intagalis Ptg Co. of Lancaster). These were not plate marked and carried no title. The following week perfect copies were printed, and, by the last week of the month, were in general circulation to the Trade. These first engravings were printed in sepia and the plate mark around may be clearly seen. The overall size of this print was 25½ inches by 19½ inches (illus no. 5). It is known that the first printing was for 5,000 copies all of which carried the title 'His Master's Voice' in English. France and Germany each received 1,000 copies from this first printing while London held the balance of 3,000. These were sold to Dealers in Britain for 2/6d (12½p) and in France for 3 francs a copy.

A further 3,000 copies were ordered in February 1900, 1,500 of which went to Germany, the balance to London. Again these appear to have had the inscription in English, however by the beginning of March 1900, Germany had been supplied with 1,000 copies having the title printed in German, 100 of these being sent on to Vienna. The exact date of the first printing of the engraving with the French "La Voix de son Maître' is not known, but it was almost certainly around this time.

A few months later, certainly by the beginning of May 1900, a smaller print (15 inches × 9 inches) was released. It is not known whether French and German titling were also available, although it seems extremely likely that they were.

Until this time the Company had been issuing these prints for use by their Dealers only, however, at some time during the latter half of 1900, the British Company issued the following statement:

"owing to the tremendous success of this Picture and the great popularity of same amongst our Clients we have decided to offer these prints for sale, although in issuing them we had absolutely no intention of doing this.
The price at which we will offer them to our Agents will be 2/6d each, and the retail price we would recommend to be 5/-, but we would of course, make no definite stipulations as to this". (illus no. 7)

5

6

The following year the company offered reproductions measuring 32 inches × 23 inches at 3/9d (19p) and 17 inches × 13 inches for 9d (4p) (illus no. 8).

From this time onwards large numbers of reproductions of the painting were issued. Some of the Rembrandt & Intagalis printings have been seen with 'The Gramophone *and* Typewriter Ltd.' inscription which must date from after December 10th 1900 at which time The Gramophone Company Ltd. changed its corporate title.

In July 1908, a particularly hideous reproduction was issued of which it is known 3,000 copies went to Mr Wechsler, a Dealer in Galicia. However, it seems fairly certain that this printing had a much wider circulation.

In the Spring of 1921 the Victor Talking Machine Company produced some very fine reproductions of the painting. The reproduction was on canvas, mounted on a stretcher frame as is usual with an oil painting. Special printing inks were used and the canvas was run through the presses many times so that layers of ink were built up to produce the raised effect of an oil painting.

The canvases over the wooden stretchers measured 20 inches × 26 inches and were made available to the Trade at a cost of $4 each unframed, and $7.50 with a mount and in a handsome bronze frame (illus no. 6).

These continued to be available until at least 1925. We have not seen any of these reproductions however a number of American collectors have, in the past, written to EMI Music Archives feeling quite certain that they had an original Barraud copy painting, so good was the reproduction. Upon investigation it has always been proved that what they had was one of these outstanding Victor reproductions.

In recent years the International Division of EMI in London has produced two excellent reproductions. The earlier issue appeared with a white border and the ink colour bar in the margin. The overall size of the print was 22 inches × 15½ inches. The printing was excellent although the final effect was somewhat lighter than the original painting. The signature of Francis Barraud does not appear in the bottom right hand corner of the reproduction. Some years later a larger reproduction (22 inches × 16½ inches) was issued for which the original painting was re-photographed. It was very near to the dark tone of the original painting and even reproduced light reflecting from the varnish on the right hand side of the painting. There was no white border. A warning however — the print is very liable to fading when exposed to strong sunlight and affected prints take on an unpleasant greenish tinge.

In 1977 Vincent Chasse of Fort Lauderdale, Florida, U.S.A. produced a lithographic print of the painting. We have not seen one of these which were advertised as 'Fully Authorised by R.C.A.'

The variety of the different printings and issues of reproductions of the painting is almost endless. Any reproduction you may find is worth preserving in your collection. The best, when suitably framed, look splendid hanging on your walls. The less good are probably better filed away only to be looked at occasionally.

Early Three-Dimensional 'Nipper' Souvenirs

The first three-dimensional 'Nipper' souvenirs to be issued by the Gramophone Company followed soon after the appearance of the first engraving of the Francis Barraud painting. We have been unable to examine any of these products; however, from the advertising material, reproduced in illustrations numbers 9-14, the items in this first collection certainly rank among the most desirable of all the 'Nipper' souvenirs. Whether it was intended that these items should be available for re-sale is not known. Probably they were used by Dealers for presentation to their leading customers. From correspondence in the Archives it seems that all the items were produced in Germany and, from there, shipped to London for distribution to Branch Houses in London, Paris, Brussels and Amsterdam as well as Germany.

By the end of October 1900 only the paperweight was available. Although it was hoped to have the other items in time for Christmas, it seems clear that they were not ready for general distribution before the beginning of 1901.

From an advertisement in Volume 1 of 'Gramophone News' issued in 1903 we know that the paper clip was still available at that time, the Company informing Dealers that it would be 'Glad to enclose one of these with any case of goods being sent'.

By mid February 1901 there is mention of cork screws and cigar cutters used as 'novelties for the German Company's travellers'. We have not seen an illustration of any of these items which appear to have been imported from Livermore and Knight, Providence, Roads Island U.S.A. and were probably originally designed for Johnson's Company in America. They were supplied to the German Company at a cost of $80 (£16) for 500.

By the end of November 1901 the London office of The Gramophone Company were writing of a 'Trick Match Box with a picture of the Dog on the front'. These were to be supplied in lots of 10,000 at a cost of 45/6d (£2.27½) per gross.

These appear to be the total special three dimensional 'Nipper' souvenirs to be issued by The Gramophone Company up to the end of 1901.

It would, perhaps, be convenient to mention here an interesting discovery revealed by Allen Koenigsberg in his 'Antique Phonograph Monthly' Volume 3 Number 5 for May 1975. Illustration numbers 15-16 tell the whole story. They are reproduced by permission of Mr Koenigsberg.

"His Master's Voice."

No. 1.

PAPER WEIGHT.

This handsome Paper Weight is an exact reproduction in bronze, with onyx mount, of our well-known picture "His Master's Voice."

9   Price   .   .   .   .   .   .   **2/6** each.

No. 2.

CRYSTAL INK BOTTLE.

This Ink-bottle has nickel mountings, and is fitted on onyx base, finished with a clever model of the Gramophone.

10   Price   .   .   .   .   .   .   **2/6** each.

No. 3.

GRAMOPHONE INK STAND.

A most ingenious and novel design, with solid mahogany base, and heavily plated
nickel fittings. It will be found that all the working parts of the Gramophone are carefully
copied and adapted to some practical use. The Record Nut, as the lid of the Ink Bottle, is
held in place by the winding key, and the Trumpet is made the receptacle for a pen wiper

11   Price .   .   .   .   .   **5/- each.**

No. 6.

CIGAR STAND AND ASH TRAY.

A handsome mahogany stand with fittings all nickelled, for cigars, cigarettes and
matches, as well as a frosted crystal ash dish. The whole is surmounted with well finished
group, representing the well-known subject "His Master's Voice."

12   Price .   .   .   .   .   **10/- each.**

No. 5.

PEN TRAY.

The Tray itself is in crystal, with solid nickelled rim, and mounted with a beautifully executed model of "His Master's Voice."

13   Price   .   .   .   .   .   .   **7/6** each.

No. 4.

PAPER CLIP.

This device is carried out in mahogany, with strong nickel-plated spring, carrying a model of a Dog and Gramophone, as represented in "His Master's Voice."

14   Price   .   .   .   .   .   .   **7/6** each.

15

16

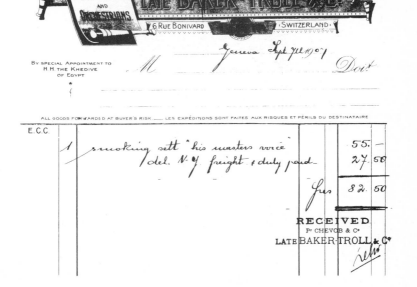

MANUFACTURERS OF MUSICAL BOXES AND ORCHESTRIONS

CHEVOB & Cᵒ

LATE BAKER-TROLL & Cᵒ

6 RUE BONIVARD — SWITZERLAND

Geneva Sept 7th 1907

By special appointment to
H.H. the Khedive
of Egypt

Doit

ALL GOODS FORWARDED AT BUYER'S RISK —— LES EXPÉDITIONS SONT FAITES AUX RISQUES ET PÉRILS DU DESTINATAIRE

E.C.C.				
1	smoking sett "his masters voice"		55.	—
	del. N.Y freight & duly paid		27	50
		frs	82	50

RECEIVED
Pʳ CHEVOB & Cᵒ
LATE BAKER-TROLL & Cᵒ

Mutoscope Picture

In 1900 the German Branch of The Gramophone Company commissioned the Deutsche Mutoscop-Gesellschaft to produce a Mutoscope film picture of a Nipper look-alike dog. This 'film' consisted of a series of photographs on cards mounted onto a drum wheel which when turned gave the appearance of movement. A kind of 'what the butler saw' machine.

One finished reel of 'film' was passed to the Company in October 1900. A table model mutoscope complete with a drum of 'Nipper' film was still at the Company's Hayes office in the 1960's. It was later moved to the Record Factory at Uxbridge Road and has since disappeared.

Illustration number 17 shows a still from the 'film'. The two men in the picture are said to be Theodore Birnbaum, then Manager of the Berlin Sales Branch and Sinkler Darby, one of the Company's Recording Experts based in Germany.

A complete drum of this early 'Nipper' film would certainly be a fine collectors item.

17

Embroidered and Woven Pictures

In this short chapter we draw the reader's attention to the few examples of this type of 'His Master's Voice' picture known to us.

The only commercial production is a Crewel picture kit (illus no. 18). This was designed by Erica Wilson and produced by Columbia Minerva Corporation of New York in 1977, selling for $7.00. The frame was not included.

The picture in illustration number 20 was woven by students of the Redditch Technical College in 1951 as part of their studies into weaving techniques.

The magnificent picture of 'Nipper' with the Phonograph was embroidered by John Paul Agnard, then of Morocco now living in Montreal, who is seen looking over the top of his masterpiece in illustration number 19. The design was drawn by Mr Agnard from a photograph of Francis Barraud's Original painting of 'Nipper' listening to the Phonograph and a large coloured reproduction of the altered picture as it exists today.

In Canada the irrepressible 'Nipper' collector Diamond 'Jim' Greer has two unique examples of 'Nipper' embroidery.

The framed needlepoint of the 'His Master's Voice' picture was made by the late Mrs. Lela Patrick. The background is in red, the Trademark Gramophone in its traditional colours, whilst 'Nipper' is in white, outlined in black (illus no. 21).

The antique Victorian chair in illustration number 22 has 'Nipper' displayed in the back rest panel. This fine Petit Point work was executed by Mrs Lenora MacDonald (daughter of Mrs. Lela Patrick). The colour scheme follows that of the needlepoint picture above. The work took six months to complete and consisted of 97,000 stitches.

It seems to us that it is extremely likely that further examples of the genre must exist either as unique private work or mass produced commercial products.

18

19

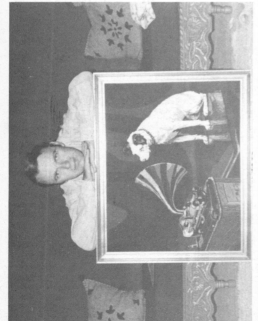

20

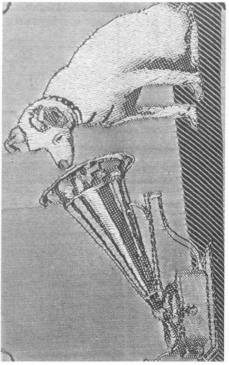

21

22

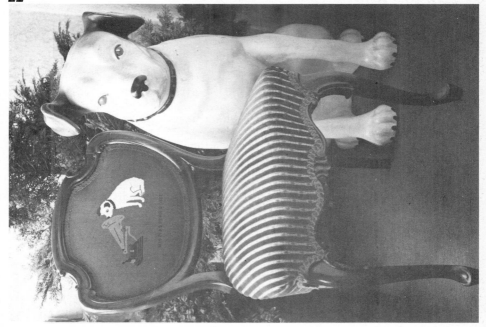

Useful and Acceptable Gifts

We think 'useful and acceptable gifts' the title of Joyce Grenfell's first record (HMV B 8930) makes a most appropriate heading for this section.

The really dedicated collector of 'Nipper Memorabilia' could cover the floor of his lounge with 'Nipper' carpet, drape his windows with 'Nipper' curtains, adorn his light fittings with 'Nipper' lampshades, hang a reproduction of the 'Nipper' painting on his walls, place a 'Nipper' mirror in his hall and lay a 'Nipper' rubber mat at his front door. In addition, he could eat his meals from 'Nipper' plates and drink his beverage from 'Nipper' cups and saucers. Dressed for the office, he may wear his 'Nipper' tie with a 'Nipper' tie clip and 'Nipper' cufflinks or, in a more relaxed mood, he may don his 'Nipper' T shirt and wear his 'Nipper' sunglasses. He could keep his cigarettes in a 'Nipper' cigarette case and light them with a 'Nipper' cigarette lighter, placing the ash into a 'Nipper' ashtray; whilst his wife could make cosmetic repairs from her 'Nipper' powder compact. Just a mere selection of the useful and acceptable 'Nipper' gifts to be found.

NIPPER FLOOR COVERING AND CURTAIN MATERIAL etc.

In 1935, The Gramophone Company produced rolls of carpet carrying an all-over 'Nipper' design. This carpet was available in rolls 27 inches wide and was suitable for making up a complete fitted carpet of any desired size. It was produced in several colours (illus no. 27).

The curtain material was produced in a similar design so that it could be used for small or large windows.

R.C.A too produced 'Nipper' curtain material (illus no. 28). The design was carried out in shades of blue and white. It seems almost certain that RCA would have produced a 'Nipper' carpet as well, although we have not seen an example of this.

Over the years, rubber door mats carrying the Dog design have been manufactured. The Victor mat (illus no. 23) was 26 inches × 38 inches and ⅜ of an inch thick. It was produced in heavy rubber with the 'His Master's Voice' Mark inlaid in white. The mats were manufactured and sold by The Pennsylvania Rubber Company of Jeanette PA. in 1912 and cost $5.20 each.

The H.M.V. mat (illus no. 24), 36 inches × 20 inches also had the H.M.V. design inlaid in white rubber. They were available in 1949-50 at a cost of £1 each.

In 1949 The Second Radio Exhibition was held in Madras, India. The His Master's Voice Stand, part of which is shown in illustration number 25, featured an 'His Master's Voice' carpet, believed to have been woven in India.

During 1977 the Columbia Minerva Corporation of New York produced a Latch-A-Rug Kit which made up to a 24 inch × 34 inch design of the 'Nipper' picture (illus no. 26). This kit included rug canvas, the necessary wool yarns,

23

24

25

26

binding etc. at a cost of $30. The finished rug could be used on the floor or as a wall hanging.

In 1919 the Victor Company issued to Dealers the Victor Pillow Top or Cushion Cover (illus no. 83). This was made of fine grade dark blue felt. The Trademark was lithographed in four colours, the word 'Victor' was in white, stitched onto the blue background. The white felt cord or rope was so arranged around the edge that no stitching was necessary to hold the pillow or cushion in place. The overall size was 22 inches × 22 inches and the cover was sold to Dealers for $2.00 each. By 1920 the size of the cover had been increased to 33 inches × 22 inches, the price remained the same.

LAMPSHADES

In 1924 some elegant 'Nipper' Lamp Shades were produced for The Gramophone Company's Spanish Branch and were used extensively in the new show rooms of one of their leading Dealers (illus no. 30).

During the mid 1930's The Gramophone Company produced some less elegant shades (illus no. 29) although, at the time they described them as 'handsomely finished in parchment'. The design was available both for wall, table or floor lamp fittings, in sizes from 5 inches to 20 inches and prices from 2/9d (24p) to 10/- (50p) each.

NIPPER MIRRORS

In 1976 Crackerjack Studio, Yonkers, New York, produced two handsome 'pub' mirrors. The Victor Trademark Mirror (illus no. 31) measured 14½ inches × 18½ inches and sold for $26.50. The larger 'Right partner, a smooth floor and the Victrola' mirror (illus no. 32) measured 20 inches × 26 inches and cost $29.50.

Some years later Nipper mirrors appeared in British souvenir shops and on market stalls. These were produced in various sizes up to a full size wall mirror and sold at prices from around £1 upwards (illus no. 33).

A Victor Advertising Mirror is shown in illustration number 78 taken at the home of 'Nipper' collector Diamond 'Jim' Greer in Canada. Below this is Jim's original Trademark model Gramophone which stands on a cabinet, the doors of which feature 'Nipper' and his Gramophone in stained glass. The background is of red glass, the Gramophone in walnut colour with the horn in yellow brass colour. 'Nipper' is in white with brown ears. This was especially created for Jim by one of his friends whose hobby is stained glass.

NIPPER CROCKERY

In 1935 The Gramophone Company produced a 'Nipper' tea-set comprising of a tea pot, milk jug, sugar bowl, cups and saucers (illus no. 34).

The following year a new design was manufactured (illus no. 35). The complete service of 22 pieces sold for 11/3½d (56p). By 1938 the price for the same set had risen to 15/- (75p).

After the War, in 1956 EMI International Ltd. introduced a new range of crockery, (illus nos. 36-38). These were intended for sale to overseas Dealers for use in their showrooms and also for presentation to their customers on

27

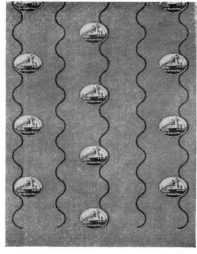

29

30

31

32

28

33

completion of a purchase. The promotional blurb stated 'each piece is clearly and attractively marked with the His Master's Voice trademark. Presented to your customers on completion of a sale they will serve as a treasured and lasting reminder. No other gift will be used so frequently or be seen by so many. The novelty and attractiveness of this crockery will make it a conversation piece wherever it is seen and used'.

In these days when it is more fashionable to drink your coffee out of a thick pottery mug rather than a thin china cup, the two 'Nipper' mugs (illus nos. 39 and 40) would be appreciated for the office morning and afternoon break. Illustration number 40 shows a mug produced for HMV Shops. This was not sold to the public but was given away at promotional gatherings. It formed part of the store's 'More Rock than ...' campaign and was produced from September 1980 to April 1983. The messages on the mug read:

> More Rock than Gibraltar
> More Tapes than Watergate
> More Hits than Al Capone
> More Reggae than Bosanquet
> More Flicks than Kenny Dalglish
> More Records than K.G.B.
> More Records, More Tapes, More Video, More Discounts

The mug in illustration number 39 was purchased off a stall in Hayes Market some years ago. We understand that the same design has been seen in markets around the South of England. The ceramic tile (illus no. 41) which is of the same design as the mug, was also purchased from a market stall at around the same period.

The wineglass in illustration number 42 was issued by RCA-Victor. The design is not engraved into the glass but is printed onto it in white.

Perhaps we should mention here the 'Nipper' Glass Cloth (illus no. 81) which was made of 50% linen and 50% cotton. This was on sale in British shops some ten years ago.

NIPPER TIE, TIE CLIP & CUFFLINKS

During the 1950's The Gramophone Company produced a handsome 'Nipper' tie. This was available in two colours, navy blue and wine with the Dog in silver (illus no. 82). Various designs of 'Nipper' cufflinks have appeared. Illustration number 53 shows a set, thought to be from RCA-Victor. Nipper appears on a raised black boss. The Dog and Gramophone and the oblong base are in a gold coloured metal. Illustration number 52 shows a set dating from the 1970's. They are of stainless steel with the Dog and Gramophone insert in gold coloured metal. The sets we have seen have been in attractive gift cases.

Nipper and the Gramophone appear in relief on the Tie Clip in illustration number 50. The example we have seen appears to have been made in brass and is probably of RCA-Victor origin.

GOLD, SILVER & PLATED SOUVENIRS

Over the years many fine silver and even solid gold 'Nipper' souvenirs have been produced, some in large quantities, others in very limited numbers for special people and special occasions. The latter items are mentioned in the

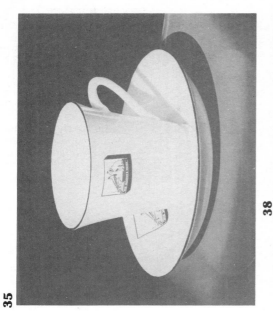

35

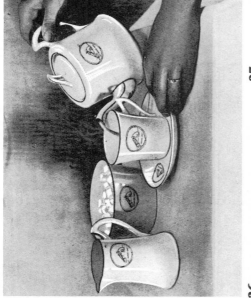

34

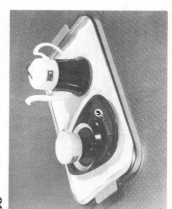

38

37

36

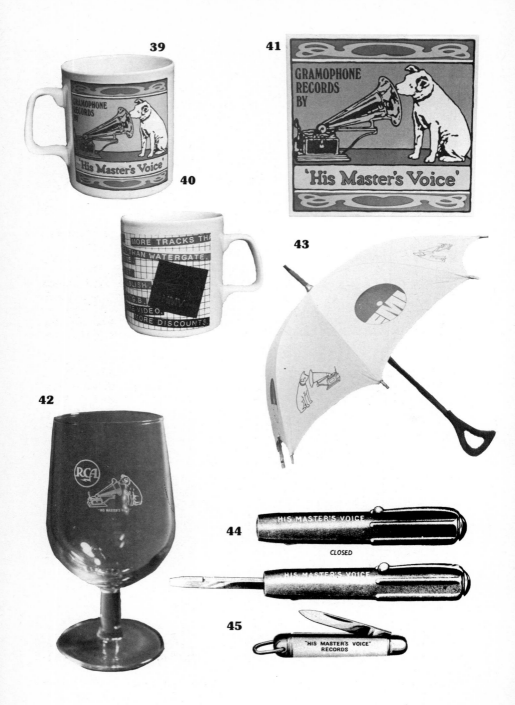

Chapter on 'Limited Editions in Gold and Silver'. Regrettably details of manufacture and production of most of these special souvenirs have now been lost
and generally it is only when a collector makes a lucky find that even their
existence comes to light. Quite apart from the actual value of the gold or silver
content, these 'Nipper' souvenirs must surely be amongst the most desirable.

In 1912 the Victor Company made arrangements with a leading manufacturer
in America to supply them 'with large quantities' of Victor trademark watch
fobs and scarf or tie pins.

The scarf/tie pin (illus no. 51) in 10 carat solid gold cost $1.15 and in sterling
silver 25 cents.

The watch fob (illus no. 46) with swivel chain, ring and medallion in sterling
silver sold at $1.25.

These were sold only to Victor Dealers and their employees and orders were
despatched to them by registered post.

All the above were still available in 1914 at which time Cloisonne watch fobs
enamelled in colours, at a cost of $1.50 each, were added to the range.

Meanwhile in November 1913 another novelty appeared — a Victor key ring
(illus no. 47) in sterling silver which was sold at $1.

In 1977 the Sherritt Mint of Toronto, Canada issued a limited edition
medallion to commemorate 25 years of television broadcasting in Canada. Each
medallion contained one troy ounce of .999 pure silver and measured 1½ inches
in diameter. Illustration number 58 shows the medallion itself and also the
accompanying leaflet which explains the background to the issue of this very
collectable item.

Although not of gold or silver, it seems suitable to mention two other keyrings
here. Illustration number 48 shows the front face of an RCA-Victor Key Ring.
The reverse carries a coat of arms with the motto 'Amare Usque ad Mare'. The
ring in illustration number 49 was produced by HMV Record Shops in 1984 to
celebrate the centenary of Nipper's birth. Both sides are shown.

In 1956 under the heading of Sales Promotion Gifts, EMI International Ltd.
listed some very attractive items which they modestly described as 'His
Master's Voice Give-Aways'. They weren't quite in the gold and silver bracket
being merely chrome plated. The His Master's Voice powder compact carried a
reproduction of the His Master's Voice record label on its inside lid (illus no. 56).
The title area was left blank and could be engraved with the Dealer's name and
address. Supplied complete in a pouchette and individually boxed it cost 13/6d
(67½p).

In the same year the International Department also offered 'another welcome
gift for a lady' — a powder box, having on its lid the same record label as the
compact (illus nos. 54-55). Each was individually boxed and sold at 14/11d
(75p).

CIGARETTE CASE, LIGHTERS, ASH TRAYS,
BOOKMATCHES etc

In 1950 The Gramophone Company produced a handsome plated cigarette
case carrying the Trademark symbol and Royal Appointments engraved inside
the lid (illus no. 59).

During 1960 Futami Shokai of Japan produced the lighter in illustration

46

47

48

50

51

52

the HMVshop

53

49

1884-1984
100 YEARS OF NIPPER

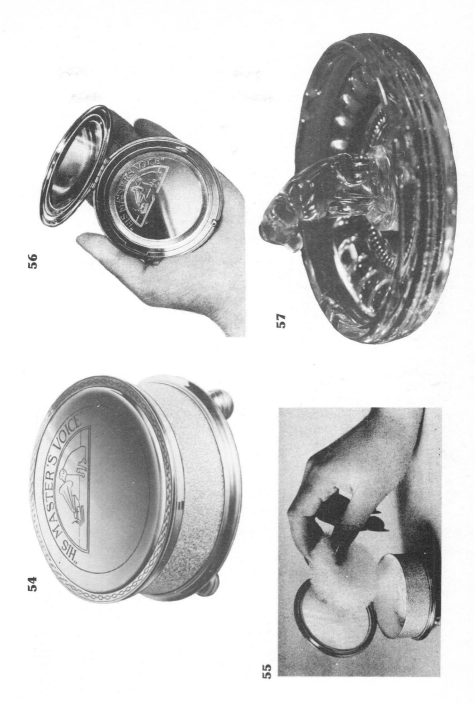

54

55

56

57

number 61 for the Japanese Victor Company. The main body of the lighter is made of black and clear perspex-like material which surrounds a silver coloured statue of 'Nipper'.

EMI International Ltd. made available an 'His Master's Voice' silver match butane gas lighter in 1956, finished in matt chrome, engraved with the H.M.V. Trademark (illus no. 60). Supplied in pouchette and individually boxed, at a price of 28/6d (£1.42½).

Over the years numerous designs of H.M.V. Book Matches have appeared; those in illustration number 67 were available through 1935-1938 at a cost of 32/- (£1.60) per 1,000 books.

The matchboxes in illustrations 68-71 are all of Japanese origin.

Ashtrays too have been produced in various shapes, sizes and styles. In the autumn of 1922 The Gramophone Company advised its Dealers that they were in the position of being able to supply them with glass ashtrays (4¾ inches × 3½ inches) bearing an excellent reproduction, in colour, of the H.M.V. trademark (illus no. 72). These were available to Dealers at a cost of 12/- (60p) a dozen.

In 1959 the Tokio Idea Centre produced a 'Nipper' Crystal Ashtray (illus no. 57). This was 5¾ inches in diameter. Nipper, 2¼ inches high, sits in the middle of the glass bowl. The ashtray sold in Japan for 850 Yen.

Illustration number 66 shows a Gramophone Company ashtray of 1935, moulded in bakalite and produced in a variety of colours with the words 'His Master's Voice' in relief around the top. This model sold to Dealers for 1/- (5p) each.

During 1936-1938 a new design (illus no. 64) was introduced, being made in a plaster composition with a removeable centrepiece. It measured 3¾ inches wide, 3⅛ inches high and 5 inches long and sold at 1/3d (6½p) each or 14/- a dozen (70p).

After the War in 1949 a new model was produced (illus no. 65) now manufactured in rubber composition with a special plastic paint finish and gold anodized aluminium insert, price 7/6d (37½p) each including Purchase Tax.

In 1953 new plaster ash trays with bas-relief mouldings of the H.M.V. Trademark (illus nos. 62-63) appeared selling at 4/- (20p) each.

A glass ashtray was introduced by EMI International in 1956. This was intended for use in 'cafés and bars' and was available with the words 'His Master's Voice' printed in any language, price 1/7d (8p) each (illus no. 73).

NIPPER BOOKENDS AND PAPERWEIGHTS
OR MINIATURE STATUES

Two useful desk items were available from The Gramophone Company through the years 1934-1939.

Plaster Trademark Bookends were modelled in plaster composition finished in old ivory. The base was covered in baize to prevent damage to surfaces (illus no. 76). Each bookend measured 7½ inches wide × 7 inches high and 5 inches deep. They are particularly attractive. 'Nipper' and his Gramophone rest upon the book lying horizontal, thus forming the base. The moulding of the spine of the book faces the front whilst the cover and page edges are seen from the back. The upright support is another book similarly moulded.

The story behind the medallion and the RCA symbol.

"HIS MASTER'S VOICE"
Trademarks Registered

You're in possession of something rare, valuable and meaningful.

It is rare because your medallion is a limited edition. Only a limited number was struck by The Sheritt Mint before the dies were scored. No further minting can be made. *The rarity of your medallion cannot be diminished.*

It is valuable, firstly, because it is a finely detailed work of art in brilliant, proof-quality finish, and, secondly, because it contains one Troy ounce of .999 pure silver (sterling, by comparison, is .925 fine).

But your medallion is also valuable in a way that is not measurable in financial terms.

It has historical significance. RCA commissioned its minting to commemorate the silver jubilee of television broadcasting in Canada. 25 years ago this year, truly Canadian TV programming became a reality with the first CBC, CBLT and CBFT TV transmissions.

Your medallion has further significance in that it also honours the real-life inspiration for the famous RCA symbol.

Some seventy-five years ago, Francis Barraud, an English painter, watched his late brother's dog, "Nipper", listening intently to the gramophone. It appeared to Barraud that the dog had mistaken the voice coming from the machine for that of its dead master. Moved,

Barraud painted the scene, entitling it, "His Master's Voice".

Emile Berliner, co-inventor of the flat record and co-founder of the company that was later to become the RCA Victor Company Ltd., bought the rights to the painting, and used it to identify his company's products. We know the company today as RCA Ltd. Both the company and its symbol are international institutions.

Ce médaillon porte le

Nº 0971

et fait partie d'une série limitée à 6500 frappée en août 1977 par The Sheritt Mint, Toronto

60

61

62

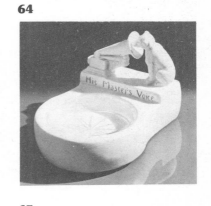

64

63

65

68

66

67

69

70

72

71

73

When originally issued they cost the Dealer 5/6d (27½p). Although primarily introduced for use in Dealer's showrooms it was later decided that they should be able to sell these items to their customers and the resale price was fixed at 7/6d (37½p) a pair.

Plaster Trademark Paper Weights were also available in a similar composition (illus no. 75). They were produced in two sizes 3½ inches long × 1¼ inches wide ×2¼ inches high; supplied in dozens only, price 7/6d (37½p) a dozen. The larger model was 7 inches long × 5 inches wide × 2¾ inches high and cost 2/6d (12½p) each or five for 10/- (50p).

Examples of the small size have been seen specially boxed for presentation to visitors to The Gramophone Company's Factory at Hayes, as a souvenir of their visit.

A variant is shown in illustration number 74. This may have been designed for Dealer display as there is a slit at the back into which we suppose display cards might be inserted.

The handsome marble and ceramic Bookends in illustration number 77 were specially made for Diamond 'Jim' Greer of Vancouver, Canada. The bases were made in black Italian marble with the lettering in gold. The Dogs were 'Nipper' Salt and Pepper Sets whilst the ceramic Trademark Gramophone was crafted by a local lady.

NIPPER TINS

The two attractive tins shown in illustrations numbers 79-80 are very collectable.

The Victor tin appears to have been marketed purely as an empty tin, whilst the 'His Master's Voice' Record & Tape Care Kit contains items for such use which seem not to have any connection with The Gramophone Company or EMI. This was marketed during 1982-1983.

NIPPER CASUAL WEAR

'Nipper' has appeared in casual guise for the collector's off duty moments. T shirts featuring the Dog in various forms have appeared from a direct reproduction of the Barraud painting to promotional slogans (illus no. 87). These were mainly used for publicity purposes although copies found their way to enthusiasts outside the Company.

Apart from special promotional T shirts, examples have been seen with full colour reproduction of the 'His Master's Voice' painting; these were sold in several London stores some ten years ago.

In 1956 EMI International produced a series of 'goodwill gifts for those who participate in outdoor pastimes or those who just sit and watch'.

Kepi Cap
Based on the design of the legionaire cap, was made of rayon with a green transparent peak (illus no. 84). The apron at the back gave protection to the nape of the neck and carried the 'His Master's Voice' message. It is said that photographs of sports crowds protecting their heads with folded newspapers gave birth to this idea. The cap sold at 1/6d each (7½p).

75

74

"HIS MASTER'S VOICE" Record Catalogue 1935 JUBILEE EDITION

76

77

78

79

80

81

82

83

Jockey Cap
Made of rayon with a stiff peak sold at 1/6d (7½p) each (illus no. 85).

Sunglasses
Fitted with deep side arms which carried the 'His Master's Voice' message (illus no. 88). Sold in minimum quantities of 500 pairs at 1/1d (5½p) per pair.

The handsome 'Nipper' Slipover was designed by Beth Elverdam, of Copenhagen, in 1983. The background is light brown. The Nipper and Gramophone design is worked in six colours in Swiss darning embroidery following knitwear stitches. The torso inside the slipover belongs to George Brock-Nannestad (illus no. 86).

At the beginning of the 1970's brass 'Nipper' belt buckles appeared both in the U.S.A. and the British markets. We have seen three examples of these and although the front face was similar in all of them, (illus no. 90) the reverse revealed that they were manufactured by different companies.

The British version (illus no. 92) states that it was 'Made in England by the Bay State Jewelry & Silversmiths Co.'. The reverse of one of the American buckles (illus no. 91) informs us that it was 'Manufactured by Bergamot Works, Darien Wisconsin' and that the Trademark was reproduced by arrangement with RCA, New York, N.Y. The third buckle, also of American origin, was made by Lewis Buckles of Chicago (illus no. 93).

All of the buckles are extremely handsome. At one time Selfridges in London sold buckles of this design. It is not known whether these were as listed or by yet another manufacturer.

For the handy man, EMI International in 1960 produced two useful novelties. The 'His Master's Voice' Spring-Shaft Pocket Screw Driver (illus no. 44) was priced at 1/11d each (10p). The 'His Master's Voice' Key Chain Pen Knife (illus no. 45) cost 1/4d (7p) each.

Golfers would no doubt be pleased with the large 'Nipper' Umbrella, made of fawn material with the design printed in brown. Note that the Trademark has been reversed (illus no. 43).

To finish off our casual and leisure section may we suggest a bottle of 'Nipper' Ale, made specially to celebrate the fiftieth anniversary of The Gramophone Company in New Zealand (illus no. 89).

84

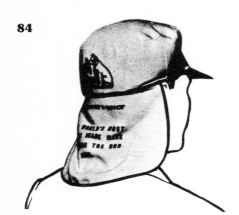

85

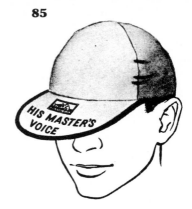

86

87

88

89

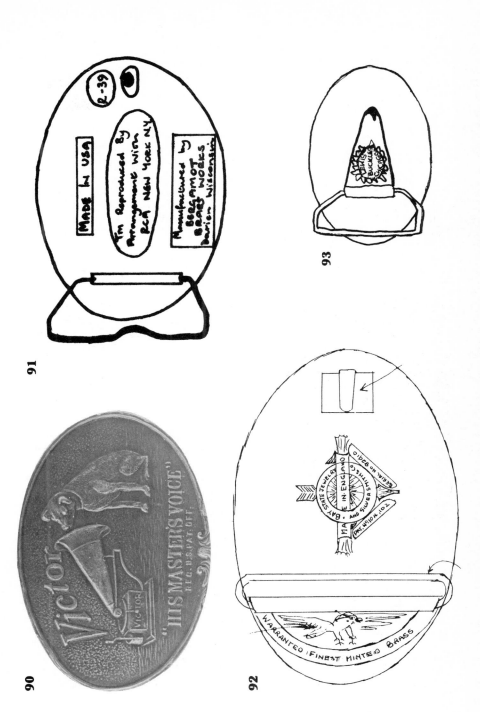

90

91

92

93

Electric Clocks

In October 1902 The Gramophone & Typewriter Ltd. had plans to purchase the patent rights from the American Clock Company and so add the manufacture of electric clocks to its products. These plans did not bear fruit and the whole idea was dropped. However the Company continued to show interest in electric clocks and in the 1930's a series of designs of 'His Master's Voice' clocks for Dealers show rooms were produced.

In 1934 a 14 inch square glass-faced clock with the H.M.V. design sandblasted to the glass (illus no. 94) was produced. It was supplied in two models for AC mains 32/6d (£1.62½) and DC mains £2/17/6d (£2.87½). A companion double sided illuminated outdoor electric clock was also available at prices from £9/10/0 (£9.50). Both models continued for several years.

In 1936 two new designs became available. The interior electric clock (illus no. 95) had the design sand blasted into the glass and was fitted with strip lighting. The clock was 14 inches square and sold to Dealers at 42/6d (£2.12½) or 32/6d (£1.62½) without strip lighting. The outdoor electric clock again had the design sand blasted into the glass (illus no. 98). The clock, which was for outdoor use only was illuminated and sold to Dealers for £9/10/0 (£9.50).

These models continued until the War and were joined in 1938 by an electric clock sign (illus no. 99). This had a revolving back panel with the wording 'HMV All World Radio'. The clock was 16 inches in diameter and was produced in chromium with a silver face. Price to Dealers was £3/18/6d (£3.92½).

Some four years ago the record shop of C.R. Spouge and Company of 11/12 Cornhill, Lincoln, closed down.

During renovations of the property the clock in illustration number 100 was discovered in the roof area. The clock measures 23½ inches high × 18 inches wide. We have not been able to date this clock which would appear to come from the later 1930's. It was manufactured by Franco Signs Ltd.

After the War the Company released an attractive clock of modern design (illus no. 101). This was available during 1949.

In 1956 a compact and useful H.M.V. travelling clock was issued by the International Division (illus no. 102). Price to Dealers was 31/6d (£1.57½).

The most recent example we have found was produced in Japan by Futami Shokai in 1978 (illus no. 103). This is a battery driven quartz clock. The reproduction of the painting measures 9½ inches × 7½ inches overall. The reproduction has a somewhat yellowish-brown appearance. The price in Japan was Yen 3,300.

A number of people, either privately or as a commercial proposition, have produced clocks using an actual gramophone record as the face, the hands shaft passing through the centre hole of the record. It does seem to be a matter of chance whether you get one of these clocks with a Dog on the label. Some of

94

95

96

97

98

99

100

101

102

the commercial issues do seem to favour Columbia, presumably because the cardboard core of these records makes them less likely to shatter when knocked.

Illustrations numbers 96-97, dating from 1922 and 1924 show examples of these 'record' clocks. One of the authors has a battery driven quartz clock with a record face which was obtained in the U.S.A. in 1983.

Queen Mary's Dolls House and the British Empire Exhibition, Wembley 1924

The preparation of the Queen's Dolls House and its subsequent exhibition at the British Empire Exhibition at Wembley in 1924 brought forth some interesting and collectable 'Nipperie'.

The original idea for the Doll's House came from Princess Marie-Louise in 1920 after finding her Mother and sister, Princess Helena Victoria busy assembling miniature objets d'art for a doll's house Queen Mary was then furnishing. She decided to ask Sir Edwin Lutyens to design a doll's house for presentation to Queen Mary. He planned a miniature palace which was decorated with pictures and furniture made to scale by leading craftsmen and painters of every kind, who contributed their skills to the construction and the furnishings. Among the items to be found in the house was a miniature 'His Master's Voice' Cabinet Gramophone, equipped with an album of six 'His Master's Voice' records.

On October 6th 1922 Alfred Clark (The Managing Director of the Gramophone Company) had written to Sir Edwin Lutyens on behalf of his Company, offering to supply the scale model gramophone of the doll's house and Princess Marie-Louise accepted the offer.

The model gramophone was an exact replica to the scale of 1/12th of the original 'His Master's Voice' Cabinet Grand Model 200. It was only four inches in height and was complete in every detail down to the picture of the Trademark under the lid, which was specially painted by Francis Barraud, the creator of the original 'His Master's Voice' picture (illus no. 105).

The cabinet and motor combined took about four months to make. At least six specialists, including a draughtsman, cabinet maker, stainer, polisher, cabinet fitter and Francis Barraud worked on the cabinet; and three draughtsmen, seven or eight tool makers, metal polisher, gold plating expert, erector and their various attendants worked on the motor and tone arm assemblies.

The greatest difficulties encountered were in the reproduction of the records on the miniature gramophone. Innumerable experiments were carried out with sound box micas of varying thicknesses to find means of improved amplification. The needles too presented a problem of manufacture, as special needles 1/12th size of the ordinary needle, and which would still maintain an accurate reproducing point, were required.

The recording session at Hayes, Room 2 Studio, held on January 26th 1923, resulted in a repertoire of six numbers being made as finished records:

Bb 2439	God Save The King
Bb 2440	Home Sweet Home
Bb 2441	St. Patrick's Day
Bb 2442	Blue Bells of Scotland
Bb 2443	Men of Harlech
Bb 2444	Rule Britannia

In the making and manufacture of the records, the specialists included a wax maker, wax finisher, two recording experts, a Brass Quartette (2 trombones and 2 cornets) conducted by George Byng, three matrix experts, record presser, edge grinder and polisher. In addition, special record pressing dies had to be made in the Tool Room and a number of experiments were carried out in the Record Factory before the final samples were pressed.

These records were $1^5/_{16}$ inches in diameter and could, of course, be played on the miniature gramophone. In addition, special record albums were manufactured to contain these small discs.

The complete operation of producing the machine complete, records and albums, entailed the use of not less than sixty-five to seventy individuals!!

The House was placed on display at the Wembley Exhibition which was opened by His Majesty George V on April 23rd 1924.

The Gramophone Company had a very splendid stand at this Exhibition on which they displayed the Chinese copy of the Barraud painting and from which a number of collectable 'Nipper' souvenirs were later available.

A miniature souvenir record $1^5/_{16}$ inches in diameter stamped from white metal and painted black was designed (illus no. 106). One face of this medallion looked like a natural gramophone record containing the image of 'Nipper' and the words 'His Master's Voice' in the label area. The reverse carried the legend

British
Empire Exhibition
Wembley 1924
His Master's Voice
The Gramophone Company Ltd.
Hayes
Middlesex

The manufacturing order for this souvenir 'record' was for 75,000 although it seems that this total may have been exceeded by an additional 17,000, giving a grand total of 92,000 in all.

We are not sure whether these were given away to visitors to the stand or, what is more likely, sold for a few pence each.

So much interest was shown in the miniature gramophone and its records placed in the Queen's Dolls House that it was decided to produce replicas of one of the six miniature records for sale to the public from the Company's Stand.

5,000 copies of 'God Save The King' were ordered. These commercial records each measuring $1^5/_{16}$ inches in diameter carried a black and white label of current design, $1/_2$ inch in diameter which was apparently reproduced photographically. Each disc was marketed in a special small envelope which, again, was an exact reproduction of the then standard record cover. They sold for 6d ($2^1/_2$p) each.

It seems that they first became available on the Stand during late August 1924 and caused so much interest that it was decided to make them generally available through the Company's Dealers.

A pressing order for a further 30,000 discs of 'God Save The King' was placed with the factory and these were available from the Company's Accredited Dealers, price 6d from the beginning of October 1924 onwards (illus no. 107).

Considering that a total of 92,000 metal medallions and 35,000 miniature records were produced they are now surprisingly difficult to find. Certainly the records now make quite a heavy drain on an intending collectors purse.

104

105

106

*This is the actual size of
the record and envelope*

THE WORLD'S SMALLEST RECORD

An Interesting Souvenir *of*
THE QUEEN'S DOLL'S HOUSE

OF the many wonderful items of workmanship in miniature forming the equipment of the Queen's Doll's House, none has excited more interest than the tiny " His Master's Voice " Gramophone and the records which it plays. This gramophone is only 4 in. in height, and is a perfect model to a scale of $\frac{1}{12}$th of a large " His Master's Voice " Cabinet Grand. It is complete in every detail, even to a picture of the Trade Mark under the lid, which was specially painted by the late Francis Barraud, the creator of the original picture, " His Master's Voice."

The miniature records made to be played on this instrument are only $1\frac{5}{16}$ ins. in diameter, and in response to numerous enquiries we are manufacturing replicas of one of the records—" God Save the King." Each record is issued in a small envelope, which is again an exact reproduction of the standard article.

Obtainable from all "His Master's Voice" accredited dealers

PRICE **6**^{D.} EACH

THE GRAMOPHONE CO., LTD., 363-367, *Oxford Street, London, W.*1

A CUT OUT MODEL OF THE "HIS MASTER'S VOICE" GRAMOPHONE
IN THE QUEEN'S DOLLS' HOUSE.

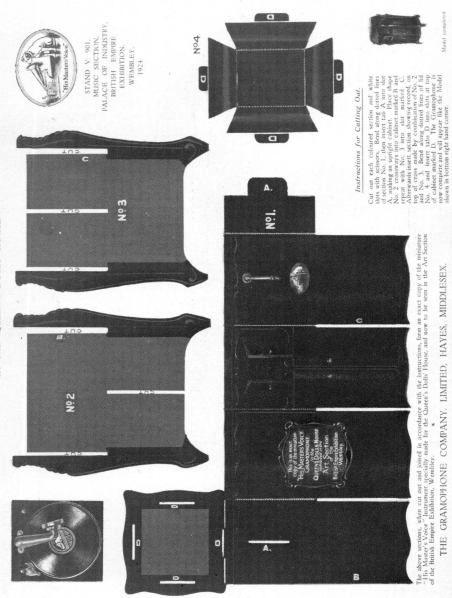

STAND V 901,
MUSIC SECTION,
PALACE OF INDUSTRY,
BRITISH EMPIRE
EXHIBITION,
WEMBLEY,
1924.

Model completed.

No4

No3

No2

No 1.

A.

C

A.

B

Instructions for Cutting Out.

Cut out each coloured section and white slots with scissors. Bend along dotted lines of section No. 1, then insert tab A into slot A, making an upright cabinet. Place shape No. 2 crossways into cabinet marked B and repeat with No. 3 into slot marked C. Afterwards insert section showing record, on top of cross made by combination of No. 2 and No. 3. Bend along dotted lines of lid No. 4 and insert tabs D into slots at top of cabinet marked D. The Gramophone is now complete and will appear like the Model shown in bottom right hand corner.

The above sections, when cut out and joined in accordance with the instructions, form an exact copy of the miniature "His Master's Voice" Instrument specially made for the Queen's Dolls' House, and now to be seen in the Art Section of the British Empire Exhibition, Wembley. *

THE GRAMOPHONE COMPANY, LIMITED, HAYES, MIDDLESEX.

A replica of the miniature gramophone supplied for the Queen's Dolls House was prepared but without the internal mechanism (illus no. 104). This was displayed on the Stand. In the replica the winding handle appeared in its usual place and not lower down the cabinet as on the Dolls House original. The replica also carried the 'His Master's Voice' Trademark although it is not known whether this too was painted by Francis Barraud. Collectors please note — the replica miniature gramophone has long since disappeared!

One further 'Nipper' souvenir was available from the Stand at Wembley. This was a handsome cardboard sheet which when cut out made up to a model of the miniature gramophone in the Dolls House. These sheets appear to have been given away to callers (illus no. 108).

Limited Editions in Gold and Silver

One very special item which would have great appeal to collectors of 'Nipperie' is the silver salver presented to employees of The Gramophone Company and later, E.M.I., on completion of twenty-five years service. If an employee had spent his twenty-five years entirely with The Gramophone Company Limited he was entitled, if he particularly desired, to have the 'Dog' Mark engraved upon it.

These sterling silver 'Empire' pattern salvers were purchased from The Goldsmiths and Silversmiths Company Limited, Regent Street, London. A letter from this Company, dated December 21st 1939, quotes the price of 23/6d (£1.17½) for the standard engraving of the recipient's name, date he completed his twenty-five years etc., plus 17/6d (87½p) extra for the 'Dog' Trademark.

Each salver measured 12 inches in diameter and stood on three small feet. It weighed approximately 24 ounces. Awards were made from 1925 until sometime during the early 1950's.

Illustration number 109 shows a close-up of the salver presented to George Dillnutt, one of the Company's early recording experts, in 1925.

Illustration number 110 was taken on December 13th 1939 and records a unique moment in the history of The Gramophone Company when thirteen employees celebrated the twenty-fifth anniversary of their association with the Company. The thirteen men (only twelve are shown in the photograph) represented three hundred years of service to The Gramophone Company.

We feel that the chance of a collector coming into possession of one of these must be fairly remote. Undoubtedly they are treasured possessions of the worker's family and are handed down through the generations.

During recent reconstruction work in the old premises of C.R. Spouge and Company of 11/12 Cornhill, Lincoln, the Silver Shield shown in illustration number 112 was discovered in the roof area.

An extensive search of EMI Music Archive has failed to reveal the details of the issue of this item. It would appear that both the Shield and the Medallion shown in illustration number 111 were presented to each Gramophone Company Dealer in Britain during the Coronation Year of 1937. If this is the case it would mean that some 3,000 to 4,000 of these desirable souvenirs should be just waiting to be 'discovered' by eager collectors.

Platinum, gold and silver plated discs have, for many years, been presented to Record Companies for achieving high sales of specific recordings. In their turn, Companies presented similar discs to their artists and to long serving members of their staffs. In fact a considerable number of these very desirable items are presented by one body to another during the course of a year.

One afternoon during March 1933, at a cocktail and sandwich soiree at the Savoy Hotel in London, the famous Russian bass Theodore Chaliapine was presented with a golden record of 'The Song of the Volga Boatmen' to celebrate his 30th year of recording for 'His Master's Voice'. The presentation disc is

112

111

113

114

115

116

shown in illustration number 115. We are not sure whether this disc was of solid gold or merely gold plated. It would appear that Chaliapine too, was uncertain. Illustration number 116 shows the artist biting the disc to test its quality!

When, in 1946, the great Italian tenor Beniamino Gigli celebrated his thirtieth year of association with The Gramophone Company a special recording session was arranged for him by Fred Gaisberg who had made Gigli's original recordings back in 1916. At the end of the session Gaisberg presented Gigli with an engraved matrix of one of the original 1916 recordings — 'Cieli e mar' (illus no. 113).

Many artists must have received such tributes and these, together with the privileged employees basking in the glow of approbation of the Company, would be far less likely to dispose of them than the record companies for whom the golden or silver disc would have far less sentimental interest. No doubt as time passes the 'treasured' gold or silver disc for sales of this or that record will be taken down and put away to be replaced by those of more recent origin, eventually to be turned out altogether. Inevitably there always seems to be an alert collector on hand to salvage the throw out and so save the 'treasure' for the collector's market.

The handsome gold plated H.M.V. plaque mounted on a solid black wooden plinth (illus no. 114) is awarded by the Japanese Victor Company (JVC) for very special services to the Company. It was manufactured in very limited quantities by Futami Shokai in January 1984 at a production cost of Yen 8,000 each.

As with all the items mentioned in this chapter, the chances of a collector lighting upon such a highly prized souvenir are remote.

Badges and Brooches

In January 1917 Sanger Brothers of Dallas, Texas, distributed a souvenir button printed on celluloid or some similar material (illus no. 120) as a souvenir on the occasion of a trade excursion covering a large part of the state of Texas. These buttons were obtained from Bastian Brothers Company of Rochester N.Y.

During 1919 the Victor Company started the 'Red Seal School' under the direction of F.S. Delano. Dealers and their staffs could register for an intensive two week sales course (known as classes). There were around fifty of these classes, each of about twenty-five students. At the completion of the course each student was given a diploma and a small lapel badge (illus no. 119), both of which were highly prized by the recipients.

A very grand though small 'Star Salesman's Button' or 'Star Saleswoman's Pin' in solid gold was issued by the Victor Talking Machine Company of Canada Ltd., as part of the prizes for a Dealer's competition held in the Spring of 1927. Illustration number 117 shows an enlarged picture of the badge.

Mr L.G. Wood has loaned to us two early button hole badges issued by the British Company. The first, produced in white celluloid material, rather similar to the old fashioned shirt back stud, would, from its design, appear to date from the 1920's (illus no. 118). The second, in metal, with a design in blue enamel (illus no. 121) is probably from the early 1930's.

Over the years a series of handsome enamelled Dealer's 'Buttonhole badges or brooches' were issued by both the Gramophone and Victor companies. These form highly collectable 'Nipper' items. Illustration numbers 122-124 show three types issued by the Gramophone Company between 1934 and 1948. They were produced in three colours.

117

118

119

120

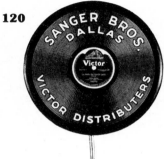

121

122

123

124

Accessories

The subject of collecting Gramophone Accessories and Needle Boxes is so complex and the material so numerous and varied that it really should have a complete and separate study all to itself.

The most that we can do within the boundaries of two short chapters is to highlight items of interest so to direct the collector to the possibilities and to familiarize him with the appearance of some of the products.

Most collectors will already be aware of the great variety of 'His Master's Voice' Record Albums, luckily still often to be found in Junk and Charity Shops around the country. There are, basically, two sorts of albums, one made to accommodate special sets of records, the other for general storage of discs of the owner's selection. It would seem that The Gramophone Company's European Branches produced Special Albums before London.

Some of the early H.M.V. Special Albums carried attractive coloured plates on the front covers. An Album in poor condition, with the plate still undamaged, may often usefully be taken apart and the cover print framed to form an attractive and appropriate picture for the Music Room.

It was not, however, until the issue of the 1926 British General Record Catalogue that an attempt was made to compile a comprehensive Album series. A list in that catalogue details eighteen 12 inch Black Label sets with each of which 'a handsome and durable album is presented'. The catalogue for the following year listed an additional seven albums. No numbers appear to have been allocated to the albums at this time, however, in 1927, probably in January, albums were given numbers in one consecutive numerical sequence for all label prefixes. The first twenty-five numbers (1-25) were devoted to those albums already listed in the General Catalogue. Starting with Album number 26 (issued in January 1927) new albums as they were issued were allocated the next available number in the sequence.

The albums for all Red and Black Label Sets were issued free of charge, whilst those for the Plum Label series cost extra. This continued to be the case through the years until November 1942, when, due to Wartime conditions, the chargeable albums were withdrawn from manufacture, although they continued to be supplied where stock still existed.

The Wartime conditions also brought about the substitution of a single 'Pocket' type Album to hold all the records in their paper covers, in place of the individual envelope style. The albums, supplied free of charge with all Red Label sets, remained available throughout the War years, although supplies were severely limited.

In January 1947, however, even these free albums were withdrawn, although a few more of these special albums were still to appear, being charged for individually.

Illustration number 125 shows a selection of Pre War Special H.M.V. Albums

130

131

132

135

134

133

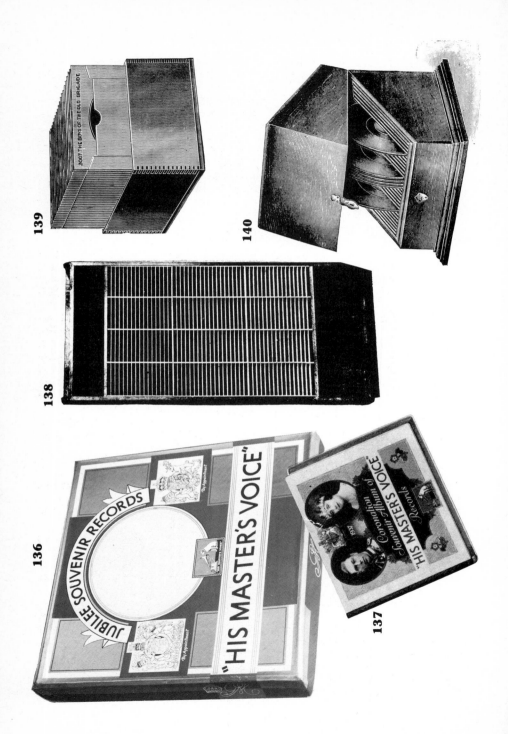

arranged in a special Dealer Display Stand. Some of the post 1947 Special H.M.V. Albums appear in illustration numbers 126-127, whilst two of the special cardboard Portfolios to hold short series of mainly 10 inch records are shown in illustrations numbers 128-129. For many years the Victor and Gramophone Companies held the record rights to the soundtracks from Walt Disney films. The Gramophone Company gave these records attractive special labels, a selection of which is shown in illustration 135. The records too were supplied in special Portfolios as shown in illustration numbers 130-133. For a general selection a Mickey Mouse/Silly Symphonies Album was produced, selling for 1/6d (7½p). This is shown in illustration number 134. All the Disney records are very attractively presented and are highly collectable. However, here once again the 'Nipper' collector will find himself in competition with other interests, this time Disney Collectors.

The Victor Company was even more enthusiastic about the production of special Albums for sets of records, often making them available for only two records. Generally the Victor Special Albums have handsome individual colour art work for each album which makes them very attractive. The H.M.V. Album Series were produced in brown or blue/green cloth boards with lettering in gold.

The late Ian Coosens had an almost complete run of all the H.M.V. English Special Albums in the numerical series, and a fine collection it made.

Numerous albums and containers have been issued for special events. Illustration numbers 136-137 show the souvenir box for the 1935 Silver Jubilee Records, and the album for the 1937 Coronation. A fine Album in blue cloth was made to hold the set of the 1937 Coronation Service and a special Memorial Album in purple cloth, was issued to hold the recorded speeches of HM George V, after his death in January 1936.

Record Albums to hold personal choice of the owner have been available from a very early time. Both the Gramophone and Victor Companies have issued a great variety of attractive albums which would require a special study to list and identify. We have chosen to illustrate a small selection through the years as a guide to what the collector may find during his or her foraging expeditions.

The Victor Album in illustration number 141 dates from 1911, whilst the albums in illustration number 142 are German and date from 1908-1910.

Illustration number 143 shows the popular range of British H.M.V. Albums which ran for many years. Those illustrated are the 1929 series.

In February 1938 The Gramophone Company introduced a de-luxe 'Nest Pocket' Album (illus no. 144).

Many designs of Record Carrying Cases have been produced through the years. The metal case in illustration number 145 was available through the 1920's and sold for 15/- (75p), the numbered index cost 3/6d (17½p) extra. The black leatherette covered case is a Post War product, dating from 1949 (illus no. 146).

The earliest console Record Storage Cabinet we have traced, in this case we are inclined to describe it as a 'rack', was issued by The Gramophone Company early in 1899. This did not, of course, carry the Dog Trademark, it was prior to the Company purchasing the painting. Although 'dogless' we have decided to include illustrations numbers 138-140 because they show the earliest disc storage cabinets we have come across. The cabinet in illustration number 138 held 1000 records. It sold for £3. The small Storage Box in illustration number 139 accommodated 60 records and sold for 7/6d (37½p). Both items date from

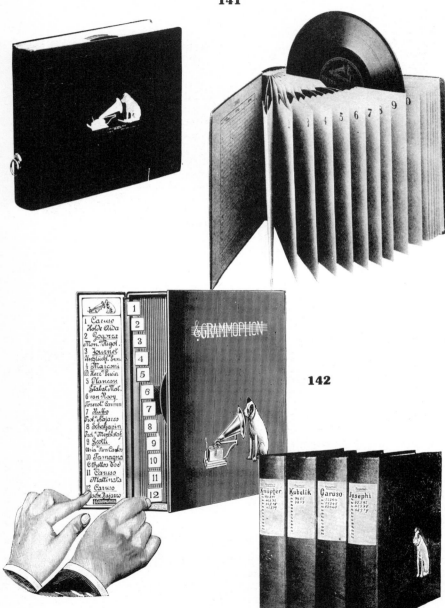

141

142

145

146

143

144

147

149

148

150

the Spring of 1899. The more sophisticated Storage Box in illustration number 140 came from Germany and dates from 1903.

The Victor Company was certainly marketing a complete range of Storage Cabinets with doors at prices ranging from $45 to $75 as early as 1909. Strangely, none of these appear to have carried the 'Dog' Trademark.

From the time that the new Cabinet Factory was opened in 1911 at their Hayes Factory, The Gramophone Company was noted for the fine quality of its gramophone cabinets. The same quality was reflected in the console Record Storage Cabinets they issued.

The Gramophone Company Cabinet in illustration number 148 dated from 1922. This came in two finishes — Mahogany £22/10/0d and Oak £18/0/0d. A revised model, number three appeared in 1925 and model number five in 1930. Model number ten (illus no. 147) appeared around 1937 selling for sevenguineas. Three handsome Post War models continued The Gramophone Company tradition. Model 2050 was released in 1950 (illus no. 149) at a cost of 28 guineas and 2051 of 1953 (illus no. 150) sold for the same price. A cheaper cabinet 2052 was released in 1955 and sold for 17 guineas. This was the last of the long series of Gramophone Company Record Storage Cabinets to come out of Hayes before the Famous Cabinet Factory was closed down when radio, radiogram and television production was discontinued on the site.

The earliest 'Nipper' Needle Container we have traced dates from 1902 and is certainly a very collectable 'Nipper' souvenir. It was sold to the public for 2/6d (12½p) (illus no. 156).

The Box in illustration number 155 was issued in 1900. It continued to be available for a number of years. A German box of the same design, dating from 1907, has been seen. These boxes did not carry the Dog Trademark. The first wooden Needle Box of this type to carry the Dog mark that we have found is shown in illustration number 153. We think it was issued around 1912. It sold for 9d (4p) and continued to be available, with slight variations, for some years.

The Box in illustration number 154 was issued in March 1920.

The handsome Needle Box shown in illustration number 157 was available in Italy and Spain from 1912 through to 1924.

By 1923 a fine plated metal Box (illus no. 151) was placed on sale in Britain, selling at a retail price of 3/- (15p). It was also available in France (illus no. 152). This design continued to be available right up to the War in 1939.

The Victor Company introduced its Fibre Needle Cutter during 1911 selling at $2.00 (illus no. 158). The Gramophone Company began to market a similar design during 1912-1914 selling at 12/6d (62½p). These models did not carry the Dog Trademark. Victor quickly introduced a revised model during 1912 selling at $2.00 (illus no. 159), followed in May 1913 by 'An improved model' (illus no. 160) selling at $1.50. The Gramophone Company also marketed this model during 1915 selling it for 12/6d (62½p) (illus no. 161).

During 1924 The Gramophone Company began to issue a series of newly designed cutters which cut the fibre needle whilst it was still in place in the soundbox. Thus, new designs had to be issued to suit each model of soundbox. Some of these cutters carry the Dog mark, others do not. Illustration number 162 shows the 1924 Cutter which sold for 5/- (25p).

H.M.V.'s Post War Thorn Needle Sharpener is shown in illustration number 163.

The Gramophone Company introduced its Instantaneous Speed Tester at the

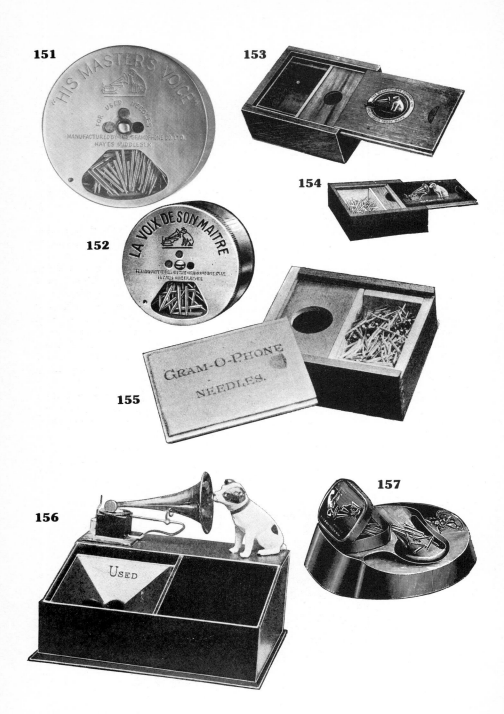

end of 1921, selling at 7/6d (37½), reducing to 5/- (25p) in 1926. Illustration number 167 shows the model at the time it first appeared. In 1928-1929 the design was somewhat changed (illus no. 168). The price remained at 5/-, reducing to 3/6d (17½p) by 1930.

Around 1915, possibly earlier, The Gramophone Company produced an oval Record Cleaning Pad (illus no. 164) measuring 5¾ inches. Finished in polished mahogany, it sold for 2/6d (12½p), rising to 4/6d (22½p) in 1920. Some Spanish Pads of this model have been seen with a circular Trademark. In 1921-922 a smaller version was substituted, selling for 2/- (10p). This, in its turn, was superceded in 1925-1926, by a circular Pad (illus no. 165) selling at 1/6d (7½p). This was available in both oak and mahogany finish. This model, with perhaps slight variations to the Trademark transfer, ran right through up to the War years.

In 1948 when production resumed after the War a new plastic topped Cleaning Pad was introduced (illus no. 166) selling for 4/6d (22½p) plus Tax. This was the last of the series, being overtaken by the L.P.'s which required different cleaning treatment.

The soundbox was always the most delicate part of the Gramophone and the one most vulnerable to damage. To protect it, special Sound Box Cases were manufactured. Illustration number 169 shows one of these, dating from 1913, with the Exhibition Sound Box in place. These cases were most handsome affairs, being velvet lined and covered in fine leather. In 1913 they sold for 3/6d (17½p) each or, £1/13/6d (£1.67½p) complete with an Exhibition Sound Box.

The interesting Record Groove Indicator seems to have been introduced circa 1936-1937. It sold for 2/6d (12½p) and was available through to 1940 (illus nos. 170-171). It was sold in a black imitation leather slip case with the Dog etc. in gold.

Tubes and bottles of Motor Oil and Grease are now comparatively rare since the contents were used up and the container was then usually well greased and oil stained and was therefore thrown away. Illustrations numbers 172-178 show a selection of these products.

A number of the accessories — Fibre Needle Cutters, Instantaneous Speed Tester, Metal Needle Container and some early examples of Oil and Grease were packed in handsome orange and black boxes. Naturally they are much more collectable and attractive if found still in their original packing.

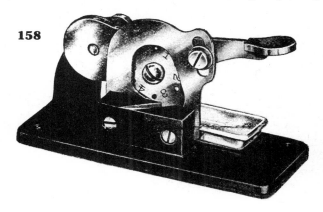

158

159

160

161

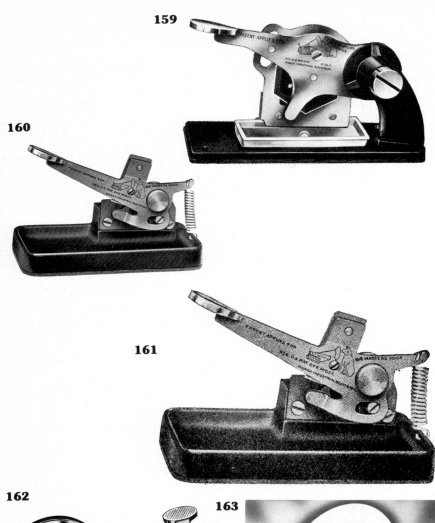

162

FIBRE NEEDLE CUTTER

163

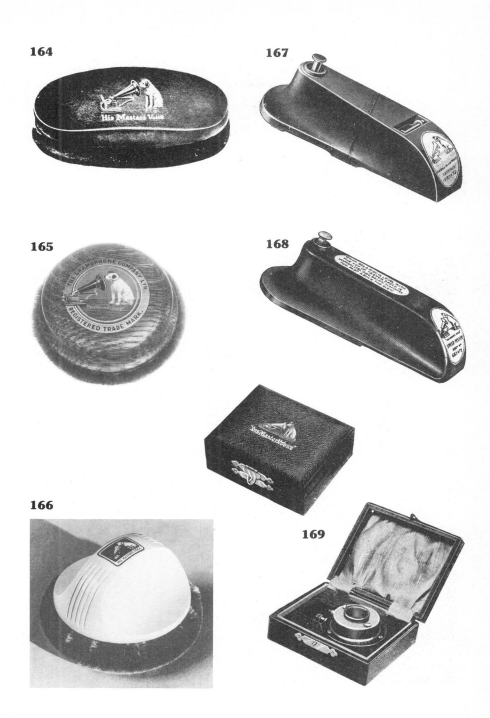

164

167

165

168

166

169

170

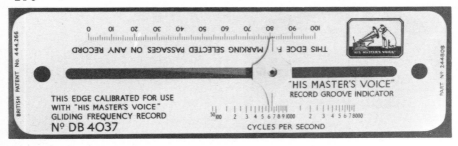

BRITISH PATENT No 444,266

0 01 02 03 04 05 06 07 08 09 001

THIS EDGE F! MARKING SELECTED PASSAGES ON ANY RECORD

"HIS MASTER'S VOICE"

PART N° 244808

"HIS MASTER'S VOICE"
RECORD GROOVE INDICATOR

THIS EDGE CALIBRATED FOR USE
WITH "HIS MASTER'S VOICE"
GLIDING FREQUENCY RECORD
N° DB 4037

50
100   2   3 4 5 6 789 1000   2   3 4 5 6 78 8000
CYCLES PER SECOND

172   **173**   **174**

171

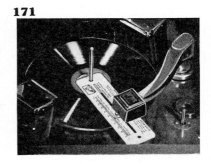

175   **176**   **177**   **178**

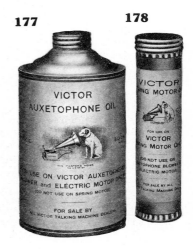

Needle Boxes

A detailed study on collecting and dating needle tins is urgently needed. Perhaps, one day, a leading expert in this field will place his or her knowledge at the disposal of other collectors, in the form of a Paper or a book.

In the meantime, Mrs Ruth Lambert, one of Britain's leading Collector-Dealers in needle tins has greatly assisted us in constructing this short chapter, which, of course, concentrates only upon tins featuring 'Nipper'. A large proportion of those illustrated come from Mrs Lambert's extensive collection.

Many tins were available over a considerable span of years, often with little or no variation in wording or design. This makes the exact dating of a tin extremely difficult, a problem exacerbated by the carelessness of the Companies who often did not use the *exact* contemporary design of tin in their needle advertisements, probably making use of older printing blocks.

The most difficult 'Nipper' tins to date are the handsome coloured 'Dog' tins as shown in illustration numbers 206-209. The first of these came in around 1907 just at the end of The Gramophone & Typewriter Ltd. era. The earliest would, of course, have carried that Company's inscription. The design ran through into the middle 1950's with minor variations of wording and the placement of the text etc.

If you think you have duplicate tins do not dispose of them before making a minute comparison of the two items. Compare the lettering on each and note any variation in text or the placing of the wording, both on the back and front of the tin itself and also on the black paper insert. Any variation or change in the colour reproduction itself could constitute a separate edition of the tin and many years may separate the date of their production.

It is important to try to collect tins which have the black paper insert still in place, although never pass over a tin you want because this is missing. A word of warning, however, you should never change over the paper insert from a damaged or poor quality tin to another in better condition unless you are absolutely certain that the design of the tins is exactly identical. The paper insert is an integral part of the tin and the wording and printing of the paper may well vary with the time of the production of the tin itself.

Clearly a tin containing needles is more desirable than an empty one, although, unless you are very experienced in recognising different needles you can never be quite sure that the needles are in fact the ones the tin originally contained, unless of course, you are lucky enough to find one with its seal still in place.

As a guide to the collector we have illustrated a range of Victor and Gramophone Company Needle Tins.

Illustrations numbers 179 to 188 are all of products from the Victor Company. The splendid Victor Dealer's Needle Showcase was available to Dealers in the U.S.A. during 1922. The Victor tins in illustration number 188 date from 1908.

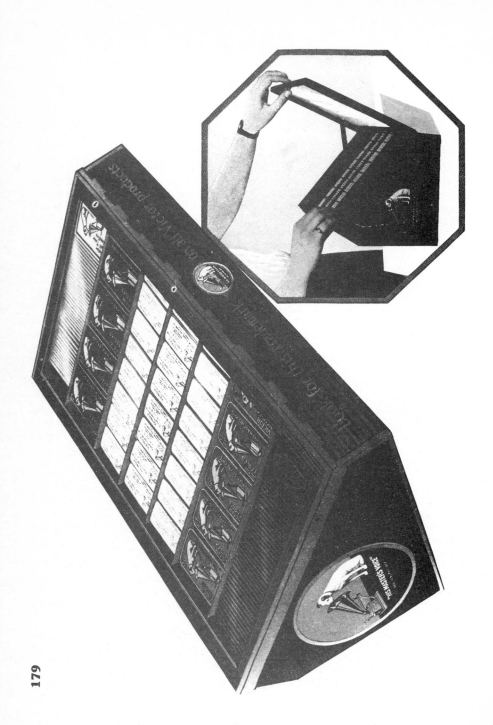

180

184

183

181

185

186

182

187

188

189

190

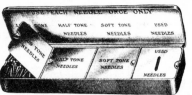

191

192

193

194

195

196

197

198

200

201

199

202

204

203

205

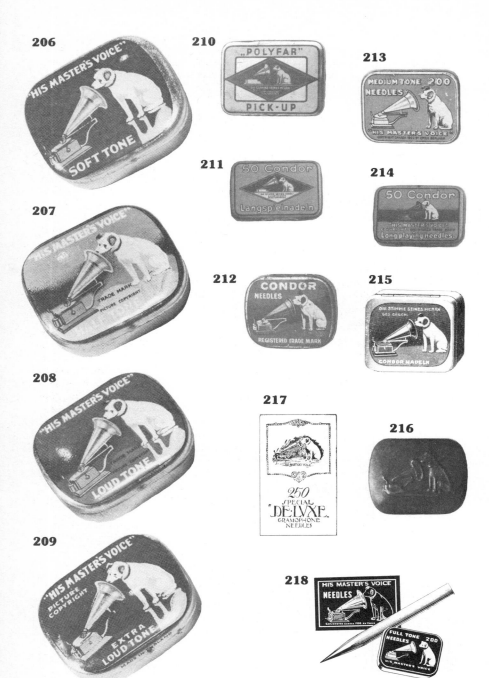

206

207

208

209

210

211

212

213

214

215

216

217

218

Illustration numbers 182 and 187 show two rare Victor American large sized tins, whilst numbers 180-181 show tins, both of which have an embossed 'Dog', in an oval design. It is thought that number 180 is of Japanese origin. Illustration number 184 shows a Canadian Victor Tungs-tone tin and needle of 1926, whilst those in illustrations 185-186 are from U.S. Victor.

Some interesting and now quite rare Needle Outfits are shown on page number 86.

Illustration number 189 shows a German five compartment outfit from 1909 whilst illustration number 192 reveals the inside of a French outfit dating from 1906-1907. The English three compartment unit in illustration number 191 dates from 1910 and number 190 shows the inside of a British outfit dating from 1922. It seems probable that the Needle Outfit Box in illustration number 199 originally contained such an Outfit. The interesting H.M.V. embossed aluminium tins date from 1923-24 (the Victor version may be seen in the Dealer's Needle Display Unit in illustration number 179). The British tins (illus nos. 193-195) had a match striker strip in the back. The tin in illustration number 196 is of similar design and was issued by the Spanish Branch of The Gramophone Company. Illustration number 197 shows a French tin from 1908. British Tungstyle needle tins from 1930 are shown in number 198. Illustration numbers 200-205 all date from 1949, at this time the British home market had lost its handsome 'Dog' Tins and the steel needles were now sold in cardboard boxes. It is thought that tins continued to be supplied for the export market.

Illustration number 216 shows the earliest 'Dog' box, dating from 1903 and running through to 1907. The 'Dog' tins in illustration numbers 206-209 have already been mentioned earlier in the chapter. Condor Needles originate in Germany, the tin in illustration number 215 dates from 1910. The Paper Packet in illustration 217 dates from 1918 and comes from Italy. The Polyfar Tin in number 210 dates from circa 1920 when the Deutsche Grammophon Actien Gesellschaft had become independent from The Gramophone Company. Illustration number 218 shows Canadian Victor Needles dating from circa 1926.

The Gramophone Company Dealer Showcases are shown on page 90. Illustration number 219 shows a unit dating from 1938 whilst number 220 shows the Post War version of 1956.

The H.M.V. Stylii in illustration numbers 221-226 are all Post War, dating from around 1953-1956. All the tins shown in illustration numbers 227-241 reveal variations and plagiarisms of the 'His Master's Voice' theme.

219

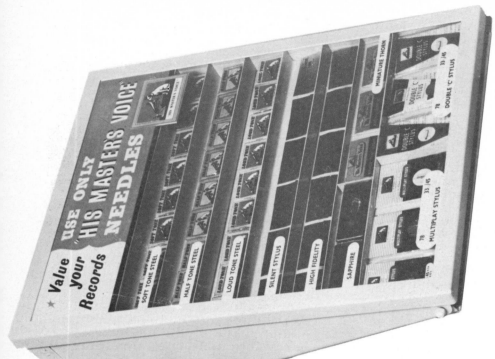

220

221

222

223

225

224

226

227

228

229

230

231

232

233

234

235

236

237

238

239

240

241

Christmas Cards, Calendars, Seasonal Pictures and Posters

Although not produced as calendars there are three very attractive and collectable series of paintings showing the adventures of 'Nipper' the Dog during various seasons of the year.

During 1907/8 the artist S.E. Scott produced a series of eight paintings (illus nos. 248-255). It seems just possible that four of the unsigned pictures may also be by Scott thus completing the pictorial year.

In 1909 Cecil Aldin made an outstanding set of six pictures of 'Nipper' in Spring, Summer and Autumn (illus nos. 242-247). These appeared on the fronts of six of the Gramophone Company's Monthly Supplements in 1909.

Two pictures by H.A. Hogg (illus nos. 256-257) appeared on the Supplements for January and October 1908 and a further eight unsigned adventures (illus nos. 258-265 were featured during 1907-1909, making a fine collection of twenty-four pictures in all. A number, if not all, of the above pictures were also issued as postcards during 1907-1910. Copies of a few of these have been found.

An unknown artist produced the vision of the Three Kings bringing gifts of Gramophones and Records for 'Nipper' and his delighted family (illus no. 266). This was placed on the cover of the Spanish Company's February 1908 Record Supplement.

Another un-named artist produced the delightful 'Christmas Morning' (illus no. 268) used by The Gramophone Company in 1910 both as a poster and as a cover for a Christmas Supplement.

In 1976 EMI Records current house magazine 'Music Talk' featured an updated pop orientated 'Dog' in monthly activities throughout the year. Some of the months appear in illustration numbers 269-274. The 'New' Dog also appeared on an enamel brooch (illus no. 275). The name of his creator is unknown.

It seems fairly certain that both The Gramophone Company together with most of its European Branches and also the Victor Company in America must have produced Company calendars from an early date. The earliest we have found appeared in 1919 (illus no. 267). It measured 7 inches × 13½ inches and was printed in colour by Brown and Bigelow of St. Paul Minn., priced at 25 cents in lots of 100.

For the 1921 Christmas season, Victor turned to the Reinzke-Ellis company who produced Calendar, Christmas Card and Christmas record delivery envelope. The Calendar was printed in green, purple and black. The Christmas Card was in red, green and black (illus nos. 277-278).

Illustration numbers 279-283 show a selection of 'Nipper' Christmas Cards issued between 1910 and the 1970's. The card (illus no. 279) showing 'Nipper' wearing the Gramophone horn on his head was by the artist Hassell who designed a series of posters for The Gramophone Company, three of which are shown in the chapter on Posters.

242

243

244

245

246

247

248

249

250

251

252

253

254

255

256

257

258

259

260

261

262

263

264

265

FIESTA DE REYES

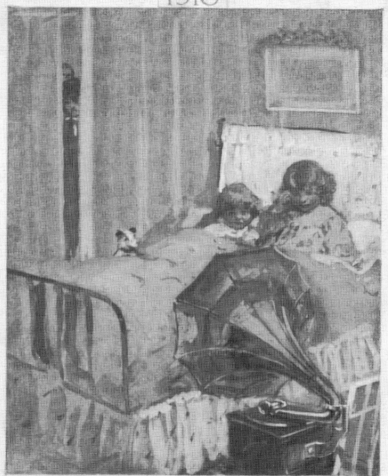

Christmas Morning 1910

"His Master's Voice"

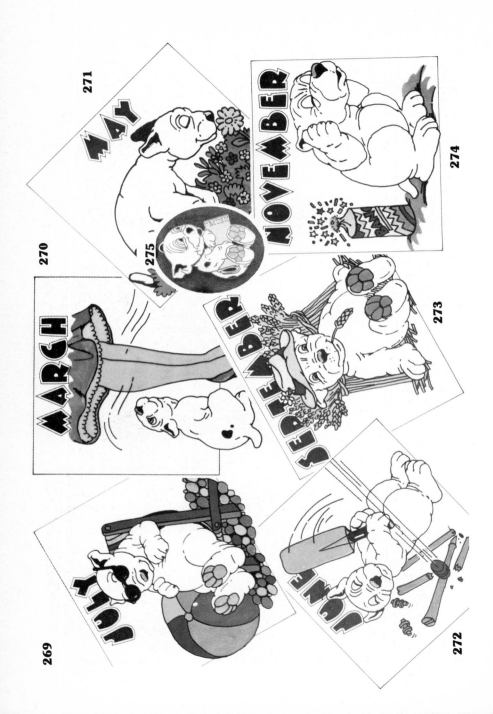

276

277

278

281

283

282

280

279

Illustration number 284 is also by Hassell. This appeared both as a poster and on the cover of a Summer Record Supplement.

In 1926 the Victor Company produced a calendar featuring a Victrola and the Dog in suitable scenes for each month and with pictures of Victor recording artistes in the squares for most days of the year (illus no. 276).

To celebrate and promote the 100th anniversary of 'Nipper's' birth in 1984, the HMV Shops produced an interesting calendar. It measures 16 inches × 12 inches and is printed on black card. Each month is illustrated by a black and white photograph of a pop artist posing with the recently chosen 'Nipper-look-alike'. Illustration number 285 shows the photograph of Bill Wyman of the Rolling Stones holding Toby, the new 'Nipper'.

The calendar was designed by Thumb Design and printed with coarse grain illustrations in a limited edition of 1,000 by Cancul as a special give-away souvenir to people in the record industry, dealers, press etc.

Clearly there is considerable scope for the collector searching among boxes of old postcards, Christmas cards etc. to light upon some attractive items of 'Nipperie' to grace his collection.

285

Trade Signs — Non-Illuminated and Illuminated

Collecting Shop and Trade Signs has developed into a highly studied and specialized cult of its own. The reader interested in making a general collection of these signs is referred to the various specialist publications on the subject. Within the limited space available we have made a selection from the many 'Nipper' signs known to have been produced over a period of some fifty years.

Inevitably collectors will find signs not listed here. In making our selection we were, of course, limited to the signs we had actually traced and also by the endeavour to show a wide variety as well as the most interesting items from the range.

Basically any Gramophone Trade Signs are of interest to the collector, although space, to say nothing of anxious wives, may well place limits on what can be collected. Possibly the flat enamelled metal signs may prove the most promising subject for many collectors.

NON-ILLUMINATED

Although it is certain that both the Victor and the Gramophone Companies produced Trade Signs from the first years of the present century the earliest we have found dates from November 1910 when The Gramophone Company issued a new hanging sign, drawing attention to the H.M.V. picture and the words 'His Master's Voice' which had now been moved into greater prominence after the Company had lost its Court case relating to its exclusive use of the word 'Gramophone' (illus no. 286). The enamelled metal sign with wrought iron bracket was sold to Dealers for 10/- (50p).

After The Gramophone Company had moved its Headquarters from City Road to the newly built HQ Office at Hayes, Middlesex, a handsome hanging sign was affixed beside the main doorway to the building. According to a Sales Committee Minute of March 5th 1912, the sign was supplied by Messrs Caspar at a cost of £8/10/0 (£8.50). Illustration number 288 shows Elena Gerhardt and Harold Craxton leaving the Hayes Studio after a recording session in 1925. This clearly shows this fine sign still in place. Alas, it has now been removed and all trace of it has been lost.

At the beginning of 1916 the Victor Company introduced a fine hanging sign produced in brilliant enamel (illus no. 287). The sign, which was double sided, represented a Victor Red Seal Record 28 inches in diameter. The Dealer's name panel below measured 10 inches × 28 inches. The sign was sold to Dealers, complete with bracket and clips, for $6.00 each. It continued to be available through 1919 by which time the cost had increased to $9 each. During August 1918 the Victor Company introduced a new brass sign. It was made of etched brass sheet, finished with a dull surface and a polished border. The Trademark and the words 'Victor Records' were enamelled in dark green, whilst the word

287

286

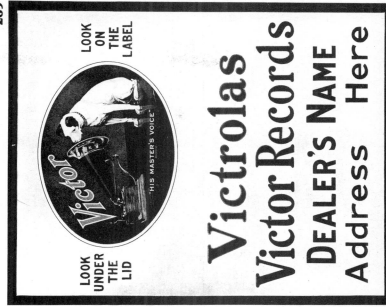

LOOK
ON
THE
LABEL

"HIS MASTER'S VOICE"

LOOK
UNDER
THE
LID

Victrolas
Victor Records
DEALER'S NAME
Address   Here

290

291

292

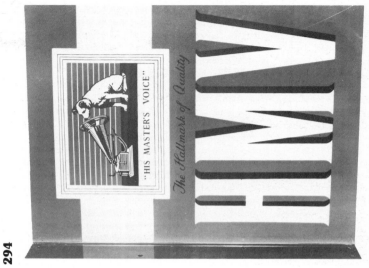

294

293

295

'Victrolas' was in black. The frame was of polished Flemish oak (illus no. 290). This sign was manufactured by the Goodman Company of New York City and was priced at $1.90 each. The sign measured 8 inches × 23 inches overall.

During the Spring of 1921 a sign of similar design, but this time of glass, was produced (illus no. 291). The lettering was in gold, outlined in black. The Trademark and border were in three colours — gold, green and black. The glass was mounted on a rich mahogany background. The sign, which measured 22 inches × 5 inches cost $3.00 each to Dealers.

In the Autumn of the same year Victor released a very handsome large framed metal sign measuring 4 feet × 5 feet overall. It was manufactured by the Brilliant Manufacturing Company of Pocomoke, Maryland, and cost Dealers $5.35 each (illus no. 289).

In 1947 when new advertising material began to appear after the end of the War, The Gramophone Company issued a newly designed double-sided sign measuring 22 inches × 14½ inches (illus no. 293). This was available with the words 'Radio', 'Radio & Records', 'Radio & Television' or 'Records'. It was priced at £5/5/0d (£5.25) each to Dealers and continued to be availble through the 1949/50 season.

In 1953 another sign (illus no. 295) measuring 22 inches × 24 inches cost £3/3/0d (£3.15) and was also available as a swinging sign at £2/15/0d (£2.75).

In 1956 the 'His Master's Voice double-sided flanged sign' in red, black and off-white and measuring 1 foot 4 inches × 1 foot was available at £1/19/0d (£1.95) (illus no. 294).

ILLUMINATED SIGNS

The earliest 'Dog' illuminated sign we have traced was erected at 37th Street and Broadway, New York City in 1907 by the O.J. Gude Company of New York. It measured 40 feet high by 50 feet wide and contained 1,000 electric light bulbs (illus nos. 296/7). The 'Dog' measured 25 feet high. Note that the Trademark is reversed. The letter 'V' was 19½ feet high whilst the rest of the Victor letters were 8 feet high.

When, years later, in May 1921, The Gramophone Company installed an illuminated sign of similar dimensions on the facade of their newly opened shop in Oxford Street in London, it was described as 'the most striking illuminated electric sign yet seen in London' (illus no. 298). The sign was 50 feet wide and 30 feet high and was lighted by over 1,300 light bulbs. It had been manufactured by the Franco British Sign Company and depicted a man, 9 feet 6 inches high, placing a record in position on the turntable of a giant 'His Master's Voice' Gramophone. The turntable revolved and a clever representation of musical notes came forth from the Gramophone. At the same time red arrows pointed to the illuminated names of two of the ten international recording artists shown in the advertisement.

During 1910 the German Branch of The Gramophone Company issued an effective and very simple illumination for use in the showroom or shop window (illus no. 292). The artist's portrait, either printed or fixed onto glass as shown in the illustration would be placed into the horn of any gramophone and held in place by the means of a nickel-plated rim with a bayonet fastening. The inside of the horn held the electric light bulb, which then lighted the picture from behind.

The artist portrait insert could be changed. Portraits of seven females:

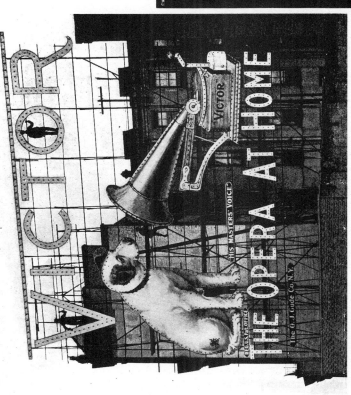

299

300

301

302

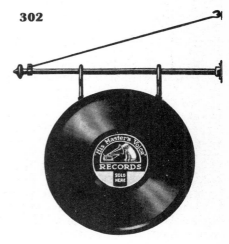

Destinn, Farrar, Tetrazzini, Melba, Schumann-Heink, Kurz and Metzger-Froitzheim, together with six males: Caruso, Jorn, Knupfer, Battistini, Kraus and Slezak, were available for use with this unit which cost 15.50 Marks and 3.50 Marks for each extra insert.

The earliest Dealer illuminated sign we have found was issued in June 1912. It was manufactured by the Brilliant Manufacturing Company of Philadelphia (illus no. 299). The letters in the sign were produced in the new 'flexlume Moulded Glass Electric Letter, Prismatic Face'. It was illuminated by fourteen 25 or 50 watt tungsten lamps. Measuring 13 feet long × 3½ feet high, it cost Dealers $150 each, however, there was a minimum order of twenty-five signs!

By 1918 a more sophisticated sign was available. It measured 41 inches × 16 inches with the oval Trademark 9½ inches × 18½ inches. The sign was illuminated by seven 25 Watt Mazda lamps. Price $17.00 (illus no. 300).

A similar design was available in 1920. It was made in two sizes, 41 inches × 16 inches costing $22.50 and 46¾ inches × 16¾ inches at $30.00

A vertical, 12 feet high sign (illus no. 303) and a horizontal sign 7 feet long (illus no. 306) were also available, selling at $110.00 and $100.00 respectively.

The first of the two 1920 signs were still available in 1922 but new designs for the vertical (illus no. 307) and the horizontal (illus no. 310) signs were produced and were sold at $120 and $110 respectively. These signs then continued to be available until 1926.

During December 1920 Victor introduced an electrical sign with changeable slides (illus no. 304). Built of copper and bronze, measuring 22 inches high × 19½ inches wide and 4½ inches deep. It was available in two forms, single-sided $47 and double-sided $62. Extra glass 'message' slides cost around $13 each. This unit was still available in 1922 but by this time the price had been considerably reduced.

Meanwhile, in Britain, on January 24th 1922, the Sales Committee of The Gramophone Company were informed that Victor were spending 'a considerable amount of money on electrically illuminated outdoor advertising' and 'it was decided to bring this matter to the notice of the English Branch'.

The Gramophone Company had already made a rather half hearted attempt to introduce an illuminated sign in 1921. Like the much earlier Victor sign it represented a Red Label record. It was produced in Japanned metal and measured 21 inches in diameter (illus no. 302). For use at night it could be lighted by *one* ordinary bulb. Price £3/16/0d (£3.80) or, fitted for *gas lighting* complete with burner it cost £4/11/0d (£4.55). This sign was still available in 1925 by which time it had been joined by a new design (illus no. 301). Both could be lit by electricity or gas and were manufactured by Franco Signs Ltd., of Oxford Street, London.

In October 1922 a new electric window display sign, known as the 'Angel Super Sign' was introduced by The Gramophone Company. This was manufactured by Angel Super Signs of Finchley. The lettering and design were stencil cut and the colour scheme could be varied by the insertion of various coloured sheets (illus no. 318). The unit measured 15 inches × 12 inches and was lit by one metal filament lamp. It cost £4/8/0d (£4.40).

October of the following year introduced a new electric hanging sign, also made by Angel Super Signs. The face of the sign was hammered repousse copper. The lettering was stencilled out and backed with opal glass. The whole sign was surrounded by a raised metal border (illus no. 317).

303

304

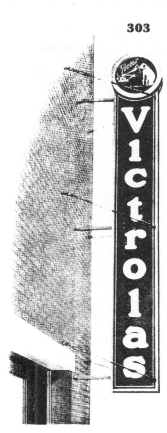

THE NEW

Victor Records

ARE HERE

305

306

307 **308**

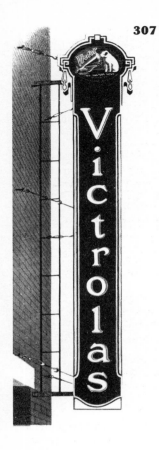

309

310

In 1929 The Gramophone Company began to issue a new series of illuminated signs produced by the Franco-British Electrical Company Ltd., the manufacturers of the well known Franco Signs.

Illustration number 311 was available in both non-illuminated and illuminated format, measuring 24 inches × 18 inches costing £1/18/6d (£1.92½) and £3/15/0d (£3.75) repectively. It was also available, illuminated only, in a larger size — 30 inches × 24 inches for £4/7/6d (£4.37½p).

Illustration number 312 was similar to the previous sign but was finished with a 'ribbon and reed' moulding round the panels. Available only as an illuminated sign, it was priced at £4/0/0d and £5/10/0d (£5.50) for the two sizes.

Three superb suspended signs were included in the 1929 series. Illustration number 308 shows the plainest of the collection. The frame was constructed of wood with applied ornamentation, finished in either polished mahogany or fumed oak. The lettering could read 'Records' or 'Gramophone'. Size 48 inches × 12 inches, the price to Dealers was £4/12/6d (£4.62½).

The sign in illustration number 313 had a frame constructed of metal finished in imitation oxidized silver. It was fitted with a shaped glass panel with border in silver and green in translucent colours. The Trademark was in black, green and white and the lettering white on black. The larger version 4 feet 4 inches × 1 foot 9 inches cost £6/16/0d (£6.80) whilst the smaller design 3 feet × 1 foot 2 inches cost £5/17/6d (£5.87½).

Illustration number 314 shows a sign with a frame constructed in metal finished in imitation oxidised silver. The Trademark was in black, green and white on a blue background, the lettering was white and light blue on blue. Available in two sizes: 4 feet 4 inches × 1 foot 11 inches cost £8/0/0d and 3 feet × 1 foot 4 inches sold for £7/16/6d (£7.82½).

A Floodlight Window Sign (illus no. 309) was constructed in imitation oxidised silver. The Trademark was in black and white on a red background. The lettering was white on black and the side panels were in green. Supplied in two sizes 2 feet 6 inches × 1 foot 10 inches price £5/15/0d (£5.75) and 1 foot 3 inches × 1 foot cost £4/10/0 (£4.50).

The Illuminated Record (illus no. 305) consisted of a polished aluminium circular frame 17 inches in diameter and was lit from the inside by one lamp bulb. Price £1/12/6d (£1.62½).

All of the 1929 range continued to be available through the 1930 season at reduced prices. They form some of the most collectable 'Nipper' signs that we have seen.

In the mid 1930's The Gramophone Company introduced a new series of illuminated signs.

During 1933 the Illuminated Globe (illus nos. 315-316) with the Trademark on a 15 inch × 10 inch globe cost Dealers £1/10/0d each. It continued to be available through to the 1936 season.

During 1934 a new Trademark sign was released (illus no. 326). Measuring 28 inches in length × 21 inches wide × 6 inches deep it cost Dealers £3/10/0d. The 'Magic Mirror Sign' gave an infinite number of reproductions of the Trademark when the mirror was illuminated from the inside (illus no. 322).

The 'Neon Trade Mark Sign' featured the Trademark outlined with a single line of red Neon tubing. It measured 24 inches × 18 inches or, in a smaller size, 18 inches × 12 inches (illus no. 327).

The 'Neon Oval Sign' featured the Trademark of stainless steel on a red

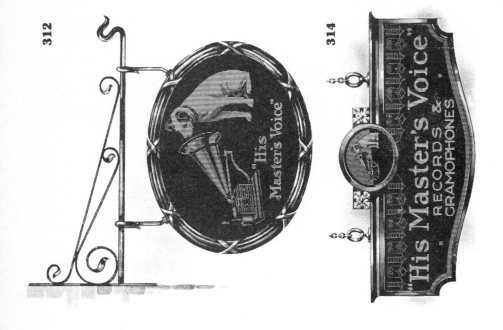

315

317

316

318

319

322

325

321

324

320

323

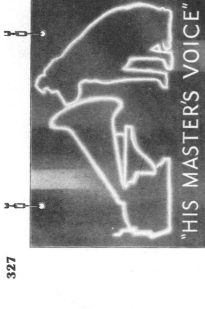

327

329

326

328

331

333

330

332

sprayed background mounted on both sides of an oval teak board. The letters 'His Master's Voice' in 1½ inch white block letters with 'Radio' in 3 inch neonised block characters (illus no. 320). Measuring 33 inches × 26 inches it cost £11/15/0d (£11.75).

The Neon Panel Sign in illustration number 328 measured 14 inches × 12 inches. The words 'His Master's Voice Radio' appeared in 3 inch red neon block letters on one side of a glass panel. It sold for £9/10/0d (£9.50).

Illustration number 330 shows a 1934 Outside Hanging Neon Sign. The Trademark design was sandblasted to the glass. The neon tube running around the border caused the Trademark and Lettering to glow. It measured 18 inches × 18 inches × 7¾ inches.

The 1934 series continued through until the 1936 season. In 1935 they were joined by some new designs.

The Hanging Floodlight Sign (illus no. 321) sold for £1/15/0d (£1.75).

The Brilliant Imitation Neon Sign (illus no. 325) had a black panel with bright red lettering. Size 10½ inches × 13½ inches × 5½ inches. Cost 4/- (20p) each. The Neon Sign (illus no. 323) had the Trademark in the top section illuminated from behind against a brilliant yellow background. The word 'Radio' was in neon letters, the sign being finished in gilt metal. Size 11¾ inches × 11 inches × 6¾ inches, selling to Dealers for £2/5/0d (£2.25).

Illustration numbers 331 and 332 show other illuminated signs issued by The Gramophone Company during 1936.

Two of the 1938 series are shown in illustrations 324 and 333. A number of the 1934/35 series were still available at this time, others had been modified somewhat which may account for some signs being found with slight differences to those already detailed.

For the 1939/40 season two interesting Record Signs were introduced. Illustration number 319 shows the Mirocol Animated Sign. This featured moving colour changes. Price £5/5/0d (£5.25). The Illuminated Record Sign (illus no. 329) was 18½ inches in diameter. Price £1/1/0 (£1.05).

After the War, in 1947 The Gramophone Company began to issue a new series of illuminated signs. Illustration number 335 shows a sign which ran through until 1950. It measured 30 inches × 20 inches ×7¼ inches and sold for £10/10/0d (£10.50).

In 1950 a new version of this sign in red, black and white (illus no. 336) was issued. Measuring 2 foot 6 inches × 1 foot 8 inches × 9 inches selling for £10/15/0d (£10.75).

The upright V shaped sign in illus no. 334 had lettering in black and white on a red background with the Trademark in colour. It measured 6 foot × 1 foot 3 inches and cost £9/10/0d (£9.50).

A new 'Through Sign' to hang inside a shop window (illus no. 337) joined the other two 1950 issues. The front measured 5 feet × 10½ inches and was lit by five 40 or 25 watt bulbs. Price £5/10/0d (£5.50).

The 1950 series continued to be available at least until the beginning of 1957.

336

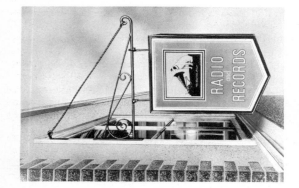

335

337

334

Flags & Banners

Trade flags and banners have always been collectable items therefore the collector of Nipperie entering into this and trade signs field has also to bid against rivals quite removed from the normal Nipper collector.

In 1919 the Victor Company produced a 3 foot long 'Victor Pennant' made of heavy blue felt with the word Victor cut out and stitched on. The Dog Trademark was lithographed in 3 colours on felt and also stitched to the base (illus no. 338). The price to the Dealer was 75 cents.

The same year a large canvas banner 118½ inches × 32 inches advertising Victrolas and Victor Records was issued free to Victor Dealers (illus no. 340). It was lithographed in three colours on heavy canvas and reproduced the Trademark in large size.

April 1922 saw the relase of two new Victor banners (illus no. 339). They were manufactured by Wm. H. Horstmann Company of Philadelphia in all wool navy blue bunting of double thickness interlined with muslin. The letters and border were made of heavy dark yellow chintz being sewn onto each side. The banners cost $12.75 or, without the border $9.50.

During March 1923 a handsome new large banner measuring 10 feet long × 3 feet wide (illus no. 342) and a smaller version of a similar design 5 feet long × 3 feet wide (illus no. 341) were offered to Victor Dealers for merely the cost of delivery. They were manufactured from best quality drilling and printed in bright solid colours.

A very handsome newly designed 10 feet × 3 feet banner was released in September 1924 (illus no. 343). Once again it was sold to Dealers for only 75 cents, the basic cost of delivery.

During 1934 The Gramophone Company issued a handsome banner 90 inches × 60 inches which was available with the words 'Radio' or 'Radio & Records' printed in yellow on a brilliant red background (illus no. 345). Price to Dealers was 28/- (£1.40).

In 1936 The Gramophone Company issued a new design 6 feet 6 inches × 4 feet 6 inches again with yellow lettering on a bright red background (illus no. 344). Two versions of this banner have been seen one having the Trademark design at the top, the other at the bottom. Both sold to Dealers for 28/- (£1.40).

H.M.V. Pennants for windows and showrooms were marketed by The Gramophone Company in 1936. These were made of crepe paper in various colours measuring 9¾ inches deep and 4¾ inches wide. The Trademark being lightly printed on every third flag (illus no. 348). They were supplied ready for hanging mounted on tape in strips 15 feet long. 6 strips cost 2/6d (12½p).

Through the years to the War The Gramophone Company marketed banners of a fairly standard format. In 1938 two of these featured Radio and Television (illus nos. 346-347). Each was 6½ feet × 4½ feet and sold for 28/6d (£1.42½).

After the War production was resumed. During 1947-1949 a new banner 6

338

339

340

341

342

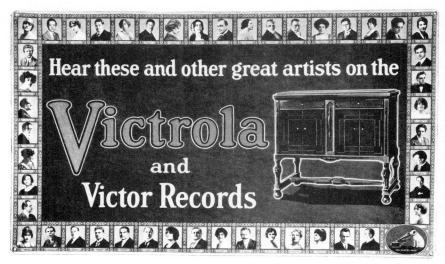

343

344

345

346

347

348

349

350

351

352

353

354

feet × 4 feet (illus no. 349) now cost 44/- (£2.20). A series of similar designs also appeared. In some cases they were supplied to Dealers on free loan.

By 1950 two handsome new designs had been produced. The new banner 6 feet × 4 feet was presented in black, white and orange on a brilliant red background (illus no. 351). A very striking and eye catching flag for flying from a pole, again produced in black, white and orange on a red background 6 feet × 4 feet was also available (illus no. 350).

In 1951 The Gramophone Company's Belgian Branch obtained permission to fly special Nipper pennants from 400 of the local taxis (illus no. 353). These flags were printed in brilliant day-glo colours.

With E.M.I.'s entry into the LP market in 1952 came a new banner (illus no. 352) printed in red, black and white on duck cloth. Each banner cost £2/7/6d (£2.37½).

1953 saw the release of artists pennants (illus no. 354) printed double-sided on linen. Width at the top 8 inches, length 17 inches. Strips of 12 cost £1/5/0 (£1.25).

We have not found any banners dating later than 1956.

Record and Instrument Posters

Making a collection of posters has always held a special fascination, whether it be of specialist or general material. The many shops selling both original prints and reproduction posters give ample proof of this.

Today the walls of record shops, especially those dealing in the more progressive popular repertoire, are literally covered with brightly coloured glossy posters. These are, of course, very collectable, although you will find very little 'Nipper' material there. However, during the first sixty years of the industry, although the companies were not slow to make good use of this colourful and compelling medium of advertising, posters were issued in far fewer designs and far less frequently than today.

The Companies, certainly The Gramophone Company, have not kept any special or detailed listing of the posters they issued over the years. We have made a broad selection from the ones that we have seen. A word of warning however, all of the earlier Gramophone posters are now quite scarce, some are extremely rare, so hold on to any that may come into your hands!

During October 1907 the Victor Company issued a fine eight sheet poster (illus no. 358). When assembled this made up to a size of 10 feet × 7 feet. It was supplied free of charge to Dealers.

In May 1908 Victor produced two handsome Hangers, 'Grand Opera' (illus no. 356) and 'Popular Artist' (illus no. 357). These were printed in colour lithography on heavy paper mounted on muslin, with metal strips at top and bottom. They measured 25 inches × 35 inches.

The Gramophone Company recorded three leading Ministers of the Liberal Government in 1909. H.H. Asquith, the Prime Minister; D. Lloyd-George, the Chancellor of the Exchequer and Winston Churchill, the President of The Board of Trade who recorded messages in support of the so called 'People's Budget' of that year. Illustration numbers 362-363 show two of the three posters issued in support of these discs. Years later, in 1938, another Prime Minister's speeches were given poster publicity (illus no. 364).

During 1911 the artist Hassell began to draw for The Gramophone Company. The first of his posters that we have traced is shown in illustration number 355. In it he coined the slogan 'Take in on your holiday'. Two years later he was to use this again in what was to become his most famous Gramophone poster. Illustration number 360 shows the original poster, whilst illustration number 359 depicts the German version of the same design. Later that year Hassell adapted his original painting to reflect the end of the holiday season (illus no. 361). Note that the passenger was a *first class* ticket holder!

In 1914 Hassell produced another poster for The Gramophone Company (illus no. 366). This was issued in a number of countries with appropriate overprinting of the H.M.V. message.

In October of the same year The Gramophone Company released a 20 inch

355

356

357

358

359

363

THE GOVERNMENT and the GRAMOPHONE

A Gramophone Record

CHANCELLOR OF THE EXCHEQUER

The Rt. Hon. D. LLOYD-GEORGE, M.P.

The Gramophone Company Limited

364

"PEACE in our time..."

THE PRIME MINISTER'S MESSAGE TO THE EMPIRE

broadcast on Sept 27th., followed by his speech at Heston Airport on his return from Munich. Sept. 30th.

"H.M.V." RECORD C3031 4/-

THE PROFITS FROM THE SALE OF THIS RECORD ARE BEING PAID TO BRITISH LEGION AT THE REQUEST OF THE PRIME MINISTER

HIS MASTER'S VOICE

362

THE GOVERNMENT and the GRAMOPHONE

A Gramophone Record

PRIME MINISTER

The Rt. Hon. H.H. ASQUITH, M.P

The Gramophone Company Limited.

Hear the Stars of Covent Garden Opera
in your own home on
"HIS MASTER'S VOICE" RECORDS

368

366

365

"HIS MASTER'S VOICE"
HAYES MIDDLESEX

THE LARGEST RADIO FACTORIES
IN THE EMPIRE

367

His Master's Voice
THE PET OF THE FLEET

369

370

371

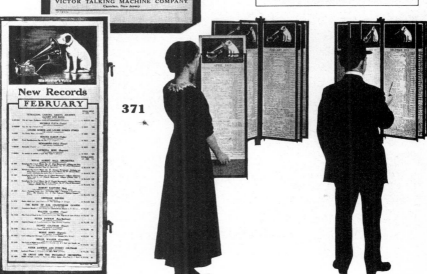

A Happier Xmas and a Brighter New Year!

"HIS MASTER'S VOICE"

all-world RADIO & RECORDS

Here's Happiness!

HIS MASTER'S VOICE

376

375

374

377

GRACIE FIELDS

HEAR HER WHENEVER YOU WISH ON
"His Master's Voice" RECORDS

378

ANSSEAU the famous Mons Tenor

Sings exclusively on
"HIS MASTER'S VOICE" Gramophone-Records

380

379

The Story of a World Famous Picture

ISSUED BY THE GRAMOPHONE COMPANY LIMITED · HAYES · MIDDLESEX

...and always remember
that picture is
The Hallmark of Quality

"HIS MASTER'S VOICE"

384

381

383

385

382

389

387

388

386

390

391

"Target located —
we're going in...."

"HIS MASTER'S VOICE"

RADIO   RADIO -
RECEIVERS   GRAMOPHONES

392

WINTER TIME
is
RECORD TIME

DUKE ELLINGTON   JOE LOSS

TOMMY DORSEY

GLENN MILLER   ARTIE SHAW

"HIS MASTER'S VOICE"

for
Dance Records

393

Salute!
to British Engineering
"HIS MASTER'S VOICE"

A Symbol of   Supremacy

394

"Line Ahead"

"HIS MASTER'S VOICE"
Radio

RADIO RECEIVERS & RADIOGRAMOPHONES

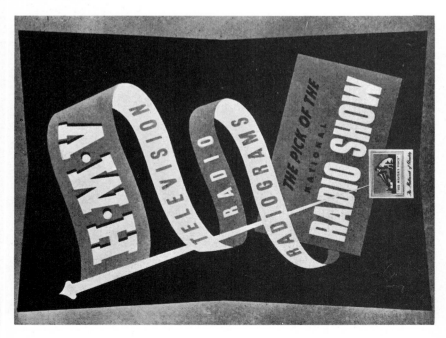

397

DISCOVERY

"HIS MASTER'S VOICE"

The Hallmark of Quality

1900-1951

"HIS MASTER'S VOICE"

HAVE LED THE WORLD IN

DISCOVERIES

WHICH HAVE PERFECTED

HOME ENTERTAINMENT

THROUGH THE GRAMOPHONE

RADIO AND TELEVISION

FESTIVAL OF BRITAIN

398

"HIS MASTER'S VOICE"

The Hallmark of Quality

We are proud to announce
that no fewer than

75

artistes appearing at
Festival of Britain Concerts
are represented on

"HIS MASTER'S VOICE"

RECORDS

*ASK WITHIN FOR THE SPECIAL BOOKLET
CONTAINING NAMES OF THESE ARTISTES AND
DETAILS OF MANY OUTSTANDING RECORDS*

399

For all the entertainment of the
FESTIVAL YEAR

ALL MODELS IN STOCK!

"HIS MASTER'S VOICE"

TELEVISION · RADIO · RECORDS

400

Make this a real
FESTIVAL YEAR
with H·M·V TELEVISION

ALL MODELS IN STOCK!

× 30 inch 'Dreadnought Poster' depicting "'His Master's Voice' The Pet of the Fleet". This was reproduced in colour from a painting by Francis Barraud, the original creator of 'His Master's Voice'. It shows 'Nipper' on the deck of a Royal Naval vessel, sitting before an H.M.V. hornless Gramophone (Model number 3) and surrounded by attentive and admiring sailors (illus no. 367).

From an early date both the Victor and Gramophone Companies issued long narrow posters, known as 'hangers', listing the new records for the month. These could be used in Dealers showrooms and windows, either as they were or mounted in specially supplied frames. Illustration numbers 369-371 show a selection of these hangers — a Victor hanger of 1920, an H.M.V. hanger of 1923 and an H.M.V. wartime hanger from 1940.

During the 1930's it was a popular outing for Dealers, their staffs and their customers, to go on a coach trip and a tour of The Gramophone Company's Factory at Hayes in Middlesex. Dealers participating in the scheme would exhibit the 'Factory Poster', 37 inches × 30 inches (illus no. 365). This version was published in 1936.

In May of that year preparations were in hand for the opening of the Opera Season at the Royal Opera House, Covent Garden. Illustration number 368 shows an H.M.V. poster to tie in with this event.

Illustration numbers 372-376 show a selection of posters from the 1930's which clearly spell out the message that 'Happiness is His Master's Voice'.

'Artist' posters have always been popular. Illustration number 378 dates from 1920 and illustration number 377 from 1935. Both designs were part of a series featuring a number of H.M.V. artists.

During May 1947 when The Gramophone Company began to issue a new series of 'Artists' posters the 'Artist's Circles' appeared in various forms over the next few years. Those illustrated in number 381 date from 1947. Posters in illustrations 382-385 are from 1949-1951. During 1949-1950 a poster telling the story of 'The World's Most Famous Trademark' (40 inches × 30 inches) was issued in various languages — English, French and Arabic have been seen (illus no. 379).

Illustration number 380 also dates from this period.

Posters to celebrate special events are always of interest. The very collectable 'Coronation Poster' (illus no. 386) came in two sizes — 60 inches × 40 inches or 30 inches × 20 inches. The smaller 'Coronation Record Poster' (30 inches × 20 inches) (illus no. 387) and the 'Coronation Streamer' (30 inches × 10 inches) (illus no. 390) were joined by two special leaflets (illus nos. 388-389) as an aid to Dealers during 1937.

A selection of Wartime (1939-1945) H.M.V. posters appear in illustrations numbers 391-394. Whilst the Radio Show of 1950 (illus nos. 395-396) and the Festival of Britain in 1951, (illus nos 397-400) are amongst the 'special events' posters issued by The Gramophone Company.

Car Cards

Over many years the Victor Company provided its Dealers with extremely handsome advertising cards for use in street cars and buses. Although The Gramophone Company did assist its Dealers to advertise on local transport we have not traced any specially prepared 'car cards' issued by this Company.

Some of these Victor cards are printed in brilliant colours and are just the right size for framing. They certainly make a handsome addition to the walls of your record or music room.

The earliest examples we have traced date from 1906. Three of the four designs issued at this time are shown in illustration numbers 401-403. The 'Victor is Music' Card was printed in black on a green shaded background. 'Victor Great Operatic Stars' was produced in black on a shaded brown background, whilst 'The Victor Minstrels' was in black and white, reflecting the subject. These cards could be supplied to Dealers at $3.00 for 100 cards which could be overprinted with the Dealer's name and address by local printers.

From this time onwards it appears that the Company supplied the cards free of charge to the Dealers.

Two special cards were issued for Christmas 1909 (illus nos. 404-405). Four excellent designs were issued for the Summer of 1912 (illus nos. 406-409). These were printed by lithography in bright colours. A much starker image was adopted in August 1913 (illus nos. 410-415) whilst for Christmas 1916 a new design, printed in brilliant colours made a very attractive card (illus no. 416).

The cards for the Autumn of 1917 began to reflect the War which America had just entered (illus nos. 417-419) however, the 1917 and 1918 Christmas Cards again saw cheerful and colourful designs (illus nos. 420-421).

May 1919 produced pictures and messages again printed in brilliant colours (illus nos. 422-424) whilst the last we have seen show a change in style and date from July 1923 (illus nos. 425-427).

401

Victor music is Music

The best music by the greatest artists in opera concert and vaudeville.

Secure a Victor on our easy payment plan.

402

MELBA   CAMPANARI   EAMES   CARUSO   SEMBRICH

These great operatic stars sing only for the
VICTOR
Hear a few Records at

Secure a Victor on our easy payment plan.

403

THE VICTOR MINSTRELS
Seven cheerful music makers from the magnificent Victor VI at $100 to the little Victor Junior at $10.

Secure a Victor on our easy payment plan.

404

405

406

407

408

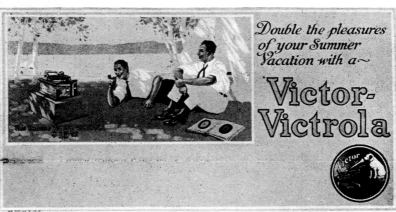

409

413

Some day you will have a Victrola. Why not enjoy that pleasure now?

414

When will there be a Victrola in your home?

415

If you love music there should be a Victrola in your home

410

With a Victrola in the home every musical longing is satisfied

411

The Victrola brings all the music of all the world into your home –

412

Every day you are without a Victrola – is so much pleasure lost

416

417

418

419

420

421

422

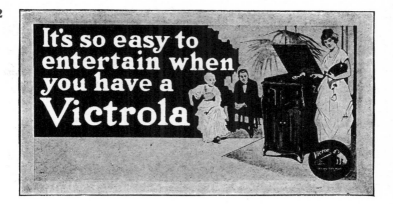

423

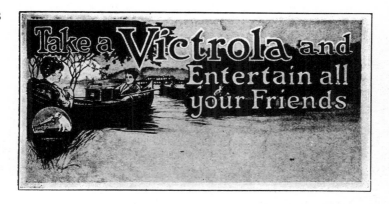

424

425

Make Our Store Your Shopping Center! **Victrolas**
Victor Records

426

This Car Passes Our Store **Victrolas**
Victor Records

Prompt and Courteous Service

427

The World's Greatest Catalogue of Music free at

Victrolas

Shop Window Pelmets

A few decades ago, when the development of old property was at its height it was often possible to find old trade signs and other interesting material in the shops coming into the hands of the demolitionist. By now, however, ever rising rates and costs have completely driven the old fashioned Dealer out of business and it becomes less and less likely that you will find much in the way of 'Nipper' signs or shop window pelmets when shops come up for redevelopment.

We feel, however, that some mention should be made of the decorative showroom window pelmets issued by The Gramophone Company from the mid 1930's to the beginning of the 1950's. Any that might still be found could very well be added to your collection of 'Nipperie'.

We are unsure at what date the practice of making printed paper window pelmets generally available to Dealers began.

The earliest we have seen dates from the Silver Jubilee celebrations of 1935 (illus no. 428). This was printed in two colours, red and blue, with 'white out' designs and lettering. The extreme length was 12 feet 6 inches × 16¾ inches. During 1937 a fully coloured pelmet was issued to tie in with the Coronation of H.M. George VI in that year (illus no. 431).

In 1936 a new general pelmet became available. Illustration number 438 shows how it was possible to adapt this and other paper pelmets to any size of window.

Christmas was an obvious time for the issue of a special pelmet. In November 1936 the Company issued the first of these we have traced (illus no. 429). New designs were issued for the Christmas of 1937 (illus no. 432) and 1938 (illus no. 433). What may well have been the penultimate paper pelmet to be issued by The Gramophone Company was available during 1946-47 (illus no. 430).

By this time The Gramophone Company were beginning to think that the cost of supplying a permanent H.M.V. pelmet would be worthwhile. After all, once it was in place no other interloper could use the space to advertise his name. During 1949-50 The Gramophone Company began to supply Permanent Glass Pelmets, fitting them free of charge (illus no. 434). At the same time Permanent Glass Signs for door panels were supplied and fitted. The design matched the pelmet both in colour and style (illus no. 435).

Because of the inevitable delay in supplying the permanent pelmet to all its Dealers, The Gramophone Company made available a Temporary Paper Pelmet in 1949 (illus no. 436). This was of the same design and colour as the glass pelmet.

In 1949 The Gramophone Company began to make available to its Dealers special 'His Master's Voice' Dutch Blinds. When this blind was fully open it naturally completely hid the Permanent Glass Pelmet. In order that the message would still be conveyed to the passing public, the pelmet design was repeated on the front of the Dutch blind (illus no. 437).

428

429

430

431

432

433

"HIS MASTER'S VOICE"

RADIO   TELEVISION   RADIOGRAMS   RECORDS

THIS ILLUSTRATES THE PERMANENT GLASS PELMET WHICH CAN BE SUPPLIED TO FIT SHOP FRONTS OF VARIOUS DIMENSIONS

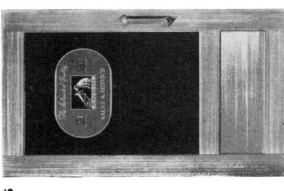

435

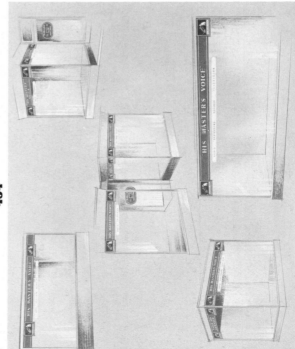

434

During 1950 The Gramophone Company began to use the slogan 'The Hallmark of Quality'. At the end of 1950 the Company began to issue small glass strips carrying this message, which could be very neatly added to the Permanent Glass Pelmet and so bring it up to date (illus no. 439).

The introduction of the Permanent Glass Pelmet virtually ended the issue of further designs printed on paper. We have not traced any further editions after this date.

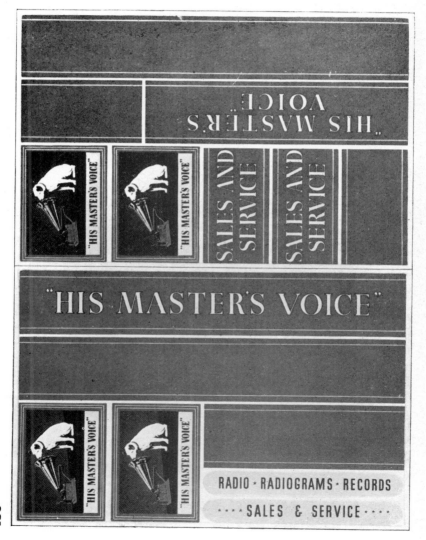

436

438

439

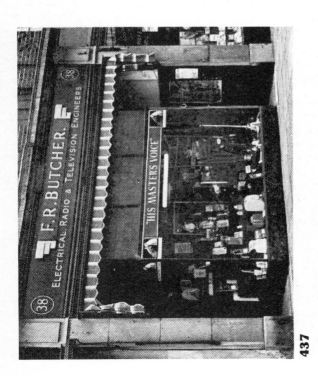

437

Dummy or Imitation Records

An interesting sideline on collecting 'Nipper' souvenirs would be the inclusion of some of the 'Dummy' records issued by The Gramophone and Victor Companies for use in window displays.

From the very beginning of the industry the desirable, indeed essential use of records in presenting an effective window display had been a problem. Records warped and even completely curled up in the heat generated inside the window area thus becoming unsaleable. To avoid this loss and to encourage Dealers still to use 'His Master's Voice' and Victor Records in their displays, the companies have, over the years, issued imitation or 'Dummy' records.

These looked exactly like an ordinary genuine record but were pressed from a blank matrix and usually made of some cheap material which, it was hoped, would be less susceptible to warping in the heat. In some cases these records were presented with normal record labels usually of best selling titles; in others as in the Victor imitation record of 1909 (illus no. 440), the title was replaced with the caption 'Imitation of a Victor Record for Dealers Use in Window Display Advertising'.

In 1910 the German Branch of The Gramophone Company issued two Dummy Record Window Displays for its Dealer's windows. The stacks of 'Dummy Records' in illustration number 441 may have been in use earlier. It is not clear whether they were old scrap records bonded together with a modern issue on the top face, or whether they were moulded blocks. They cost the Dealer Marks 1.25.

Illustration number 444 shows a new Record Cube Display. We do not know whether the records were moulded into the cube or whether they were interchangeable. The idea was to place the cube on the turntable of any Gramophone which was then set playing at its slowest speed, thus revealing all of the records.

In 1912 The Gramophone Company, although worried that the 'Dummy Record' might, in some situations, be sold in mistake for the genuine article, considered using cardboard replica records for use in Dealers windows. Later, experiments were made using a metal core for the display records.

In October 1919 the Ed. Usoskin Company of New York City introduced a novel window display service for Dealers. It featured 12 new records a month listed on highly coloured posters together with specially printed record stands and price cards. A new design and colour scheme was adopted each month. In addition they offered a very fine cardboard imitation record to be used in the display at 15 cents each, or $3.35 for a box containing 24 records with assorted labels. These were very natural looking and were intended to save damage to real records (illus nos. 442-443).

About 1927 the Victor Company produced a large cardboard Red Seal Record of the Philadelphia Orchestra's recording of 'Blue Danube'. This was

441

443

442

440

444

445

446

10 in. RECORDS.

XX.1	Reginald Foort Zampa Overture. . ..	BD.679
	Paul Robeson " Trees "	B.8830
XX.2	Geraldo and his Orch. " Deep Purple "	BD.689
	Barnabas von Geczy and his Orch " Puszta "	B.8395
XX.3	Jack Hylton and his Orch. " Down South "	BD.603
	Benny Goodman Quartet Opus ½ ..	B.8851
XX.4	Louis Levy and his Orch. Mikado Selection	BD.653
	Allan Jones " Donkey Serenade " ..	B.8714
XX.5	Black Dyke Mills Band " Turkish Patrol "	BD.599
	London Palladium Orchestra	
	" Spirit of Youth "—March ..	B.8662
XX.6	Callender's Senior Band " Amparito Roca "	BD.513
	Jeanette MacDonald & Nelson Eddy	
	" Will You Remember " ..	DA.1559

12 in. RECORDS.

XW.1	Peter Dawson " The Floral Dance " ..	C.2698
	Stokowski Hungarian Rhapsody No. 2 ..	DB.3086
XW.2	Webster Booth & Joan Cross " Lovely Maid "	C.3053
	Gigli " Your Tiny Hand " (Boheme) .,	DB.1538
XW.3	Paul Whiteman and his Orchestra	
	" Rhapsody in Blue " ..	C.1395
	Caruso " On with the Motley " ..	DB.1802
XW.4	Kentucky Minstrels " In the Gloaming "	C.3001
	Toscanini " Invitation to the Waltz " ..	DB.3542
XW.5	Viennese Waltz Orch. " Immortal Strauss "	C.2882
	Elisabeth Schumann " Ave Maria " (Schubert)	DB.2291
XW.6	Ernest Lough " Hear My Prayer " ..	C.1329
	Coldstream Guards " Sousa Medley " ..	C.2958

intended for window display and it is said that it resulted in sales of over 100,000 copies of the actual record.

As a result of this success, in 1928 the Victor Company produced a 30 inch diameter record, made of steel, having a label of 15 inches in diameter which could be quickly and easily changed (illus no. 445). This giant record was supplied to Dealers at a cost of $4.50, the label service (twelve a year) was free. Truly a stupendous find for the collector of today.

In 1939 The Gramophone Company began a new service of 'Dummy' records. In appearance these were identical to the standard record but pressed from a thermo-plastic material, having a greater resistance to heat. At first it was proposed to issue a label service which would enable a Dealer to update his display discs with current titles. However, this was rejected in favour of plans to issue new additions of popular records as required.

The first issue in 1939 consisted of six 10 inch and six 12 inch discs. Each set of twelve records, boxed, cost the Dealer 5/- (25p). Illustration number 446 gives a complete list of the titles available in the first release. Each record appeared with the normal standard H.M.V. record label, although the style of type face for the title and artist was changed to give better visual impact.

Window Display Material

There is an almost endless supply of display cards and link material from both the Victor and Gramophone Companies. It is possible here to draw the reader's attention to only a few of the more attractive items.

In November 1908 the Victor Company announced two new 'Window Easels' (illus nos. 447-448). These were 38 inches high and 28½ inches wide and were lithograph printed in vivid colours. Any copies now found would be worthy of retention.

In April 1911 the Victor Company produced the first of a series of 'splendiferous' window displays. This was known as the 'Victor Grand Opera Window Display'. The great proscenium arch of the Old Metropolitan Opera House was reproduced in miniature, an exact copy both in design and colour. The proscenium arch was 5 feet wide whilst the backdrop depicted a birdseye view of the Victor factories. The figures (17 inches high) were of famous Victor recording artists (illus no. 449). The complete display sold to Dealers at only $5 complete.

During February 1912 the Victor Company issued their 'Display Card No. 8' (illus no. 451) depicting Caruso singing his famous aria from Elisir D'Amore. The card is almost a miniature theatre with a beautifully coloured proscenium arch (note 'Nipper' at the centre top) with wings and backcloth. This card cost Dealers 50 cents each.

By November 1912 Victor had excelled even their past efforts and produced a 'Victor Stage Window Display'. Illustration number 450 will help to explain the workings of this splendid unit. We quote from Victor's explanatory text:

"The whole window consists of the theatre as you seen it in figure No. 2, in front of which is a handsome plush drapery, so arranged as to give the observer the effect of looking down on the stage and the orchestra from a box. A figure of a lady in evening dress, lorgnette in hand, occupies the foreground. The miniature stage is operated entirely by electricity. When the current is turned on, the stage and the footlights are lighted and the motor which operates the display set in motion.

Figure 1 shows the theatre with the curtain down. In bold lettering it carries the legend 'with a Victor — Victrola you may have right in your home' — then as the curtain rises there appears a scene from 'Faust' and the announcement 'Grand Opera — Faust' finishes the incomplete sentence on the drop curtain. This scene is presented with all the charm and effect of stage lighting for a minute or so, then the curtain is lowered, stays down for a minute and raises a second time to display, for instance, a scene from light opera, and so on until six different scenes have been shown, when it reappears automatically as long as you leave the current turned on.

All this is controlled automatically, the raising and lowering of the curtain and the changing of the scene. You have nothing to do but turn on the

448

447

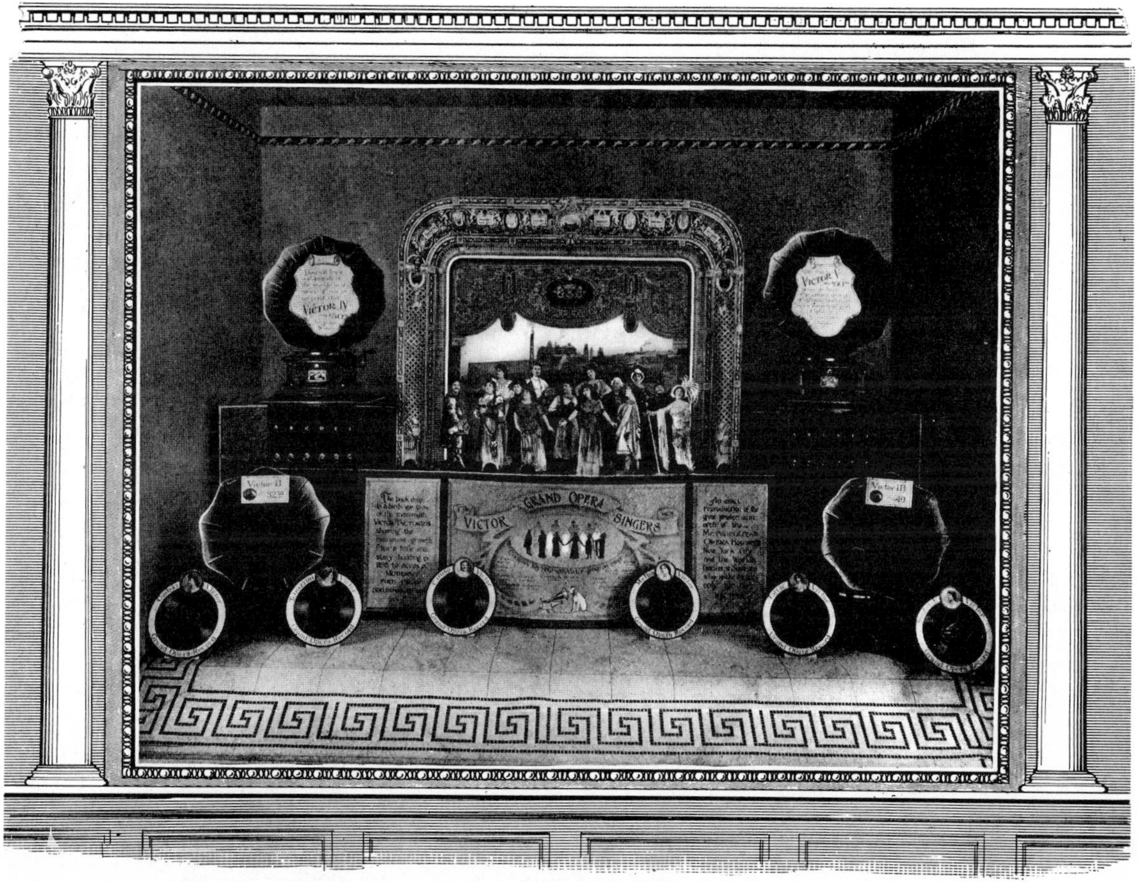
VICTOR IV
VICTOR V
VICTOR
GRAND OPERA
SINGERS

1

4

3

2

5

6

current. Figure 1 shows the stage portion of the display only, with the curtain down. (Note 'Nipper' on the right hand bottom corner of the curtain). Figure 2, the same with the curtain up. Figure 3 shows the relation of the proscenium and the arrangement of the scenes. Figure 4 a side view showing the motor. Figure 5, the same, but from the opposite side. Figure 6, just the arrangement of the scenes taken from directly behind the window. The window is furnished complete in every detail except that of incandescent globes. Six scenes are furnished with it. Six other scenes can be furnished immediately and still other scenes will be forthcoming every month. Use it as a window display as long as it serves its purpose, then with new scenes, make it a feature of your concert room. It requires for operation a space seven feet or more wide, seven feet deep, and eight feet high. Your monogram, provided it does not exceed two or three letters, will be embroidered on the outside drapery. The cost of the window complete is $75. We can furnish these windows in very limited quantities. One lot of twenty-five will be ready by November 1st; a second lot of 25 by November 20th.

In October 1913 the idea was further developed with Victor's "New Theatre Window Display'. Because of its ingenious double proscenium this could be viewed by customers inside the store at the same time as being seen by people outside on the pavement (illus no. 452). Victor's description of this unit states:

"figure 1 shows the front of the display with the central part closed. Figure 2 shows the central part open, giving a view of the stage with a scene from 'The Merry Widow'; also the audience, orchestra and boxes. These are all hand-painted in natural colours. Please note that the hand-lettered sign in the frame on the left side of the display is different from that shown in Fig. 1. There are six of these signs, one for each scene, fastened to a hexagonal frame which revolves at the same time the scene changes. The sign shown with each scene bears the name of the opera from which the scene is taken and some excellent copy, advertising the Victor opera records. Figure 3 is a side view showing the rear proscenium frame, hexagonal sign frame, motor, illuminating lights and the arrangement of the scenes. Figure 4 is a view of the opposite side and shows more clearly how the curtains of the two prosceniums are operated.

The theatre front is hand-painted in dark green — exactly like the New Amsterdam Theatre in New York — and the rest is finished in gold, making one of the handsomest fronts imaginable.

The window is furnished complete as shown with the exception of incandescent globes. Six scenes are furnished with it.

The display requires a space seven and one half feet wide, seven and one half feet deep, and eight feet high.

The cost of the window complete is $125.00. A good investment you will agree, when you consider the interest it will create in opera and opera records and the publicity it will give your store for a practically unlimited time".

Meanwhile in England The Gramophone Company too was thinking of mechanical window displays. In January 1913 it was suggested that estimates should be obtained for a window display unit having a table grand hornless gramophone fitted with an electric motor to automatically close and open the lid and front doors, revolve the turntable with a record on it and move the arm

1

452

2

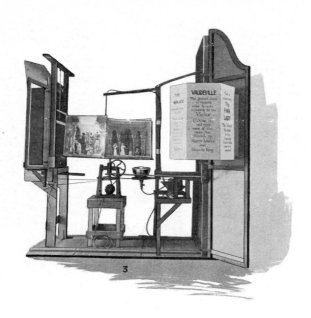

3

452 cont.

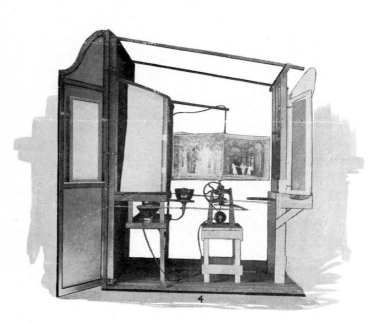

4

454

455

"His Master's Voice"

TRUE-TO-LIFE RADIO

453

"HIS MASTER'S VOICE"
REG U.S. PAT. OFF. U.S.A.

New Victor Records

and sound box as though it were playing a record at the ordinary speed, and when the lid closes, the Dog Trademark to rise from behind and to appear as if resting on the top of the machine. The motor to be such as to be connected with an ordinary electric light point. It is not known whether this ever reached construction stage. It does however show that the European side were also awake to the benefits of an animated window display.

In April 1925 the Victor Company produced a new 'His Master's Voice' picture window card (illus no. 453) which would be an attractive item for collectors today.

Some nine years later the British Gramophone Company produced a handsome Trademark showcard (illus no. 455) printed in full colour with a gold band at the top and base. It measured 16⅞ inches × 21¾ inches and was supplied free to Dealers.

The same year (1934) the Company produced a bronze coloured plaque with the Trademark Picture in relief (illus no. 454). It measured 22½ inches × 14 inches and sold to Dealers for 25/- (£1.25) each.

Both units continued through to the beginning of the War in 1939.

Just before the War (1939-45) The Gramophone Company issued a whole series of new showroom display material, much of which was still in circulation well after the War was over:

The Record Pedestal (illus no. 456) 4 feet 10 inches × 1 foot 1 inch cost 5/- (25p).

The Wall Frame (illus no. 458) was made to accommodate two Hanger Posters and two records 10 inch or 12 inch size. Measuring 2 feet 9½ inches × 3 feet 2½ inches it cost 15/- (75p).

Another Wall Frame (illus no. 457) measured 1 foot 11½ inches × 5 feet 3½ inches and cost 12/6d (62½p).

A Record Rack for use along the front of the showroom window (illus no. 459) measured 1 foot 4 inches × 4 feet 6 inches, was priced at 5/- (25p).

Post War brought perspex into use for displays (illus no. 465). This new display measured 15½ inches × 10½ inches and cost Dealers £1/1/0d (£1.05). It was available with the alternative wording 'Radio Television Sales & Service'.

During 1949-50 The Gramophone Company issued 'His Master's Voice' Trademark Circles in 4 feet, 5 feet and 6 feet diameter sizes (illus nos. 460-461). These were available to Dealers on loan.

Another large display of the same period (illus no. 462) measured 4 feet 2 inches × 3 feet 9½ inches and was suitable for fixing to showroom walls etc. The same design was also available in a 4 feet diameter circle.

1953 was a good year for special display material in Britain due to the Coronation of H.M. Queen Elizabeth II. The Gramophone Company issued a new handsome Embossed Showcard of the 'His Master's Voice' Trademark which was issued free to Dealers. It measured 27 inches × 18 inches (illus no. 466).

During 1956 a new version of the Circle Trademark Plaque (illus no. 463) was produced. This measured 4 feet in diameter.

A new 'Oblong Plaque' (illus no. 467) was available at the same time. This was designed for spaces where depth was restricted. It measured 3 feet 6 inches × 2 feet. Both displays sold to Dealers for £2/10/0d (£2.50) each.

The same year a new 'His Master's Voice prestige Showcard' (illus no. 464) became available. This was a high quality embossed reproduction of the Trade Mark Picture. It was issued free to Dealers.

456

457

458

459

460

461

462

463

464

465

466

467

Small Cardboard Record/ Display Stands and Price Tickets

This chapter should be read in conjunction with that devoted to Window Display material. Machine Collectors, who love to proudly display their Gramophones, will delight in the acquisition of some of the attractive H.M.V. Price Ticket Holders into which they could insert their own information slips.

We are uncertain when the production of special Price Ticket Holders was introduced by The Gramophone Company. The earliest we have traced comes from 1934. Illustration number 469 dates from 1934; it was printed in five colours and small slip-in price cards were available for all H.M.V. models.

A new design was introduced in 1935. It was printed in black and orange. A special holder was produced for the Coronation of 1937 (illus no. 472) whilst illustration number 468 was the standard design for that year.

Post War designs were particularly attractive. Illustration number 471 dates from 1946/47. The embossed card was printed in two colours. The individual price slips were gummed and were stuck onto the card. Illustration number 474 ran through 1947-1950. The Trademark was reproduced in its original colours.

In September 1950 a new holder was released (illus no. 475). The H.M.V. picture was again printed in its original colours and surrounded by a gilt frame on a red background. The design was embossed on the card which was given a porcelain finish.

The small cardboard record display stands are also very useful for the private gramophone museum or display case.

An early example, from 1922, was manufactured by The Con Planck Studios of Covent Garden, London (illus no. 476). It cost Dealers 7/6d for each stand.

In 1934 a novel cut out record stand (illus no. 477) was released. It tied up with the 'Record of the Month' sales campaign. The same year the attractive stand in illustration number 470 was also issued.

The stand shown in illustration number 478 was released in 1938. It was available with pictures of Gigli, Toscanini, Robeson, Kreisler, E. Schumann and Schnabel. It measured 18½ inches × 17½ inches.

Illustration numbers 480-484 show some wartime items, dating from 1940/41. The Record Stands took actual records. The 'V' sign was sold to Dealers for 15/- (75p) and displayed seven 10 inch records. It measured 3 feet 10 inches × 3 feet 3 inches.

The two small stands (illus nos. 480-484) had interchangeable slips for record titles and artists. They accommodated one record each.

In 1947 the show card in illustration number 479 was amongst the first of a new series of display material to be released by The Gramophone Company.

468

13 GUINEAS
DECEMBER 5/-
"HIS MASTER'S VOICE"
RADIO

469

HIS MASTER'S VOICE
TRUE TO LIFE
RADIO AND RADIOGRAMOPHONES

470

"His Master's Voice"
THE MUSIC YOU SELECT YOURSELF

471

H.M.V.
"HIS MASTER'S VOICE"
PORTABLE GRAMOPHONE
Model 102
£8-17-6
PLUS £1-18-6 PURCHASE TAX
"HIS MASTER'S VOICE"

472

"HIS MASTER'S VOICE"
CORONATION Year RADIO
SIX-VALVE ALL-WORLD SUPERHET
FOR A.C. MAINS
12 GUINEAS

473

H·M·V
8-VALVE 5-WAVEBAND
AUTO-RADIOGRAM
For A.C. Mains
MODEL 1611
PRICE 152 GUINEAS
(TAX PAID)
"HIS MASTER'S VOICE"
The Hallmark of Quality

474

"HIS MASTER'S VOICE"
4-VALVE
SELF-CONTAINED BATTERY SUPERHET
MODEL 1407
£25-11-0
(INCLUDING PURCHASE TAX)

475

"HIS MASTER'S VOICE"
The Hallmark of Quality
COMBINED TELEVISION RECEIVER AND
AUTO-RADIOGRAM INCORPORATING 15 EMISCOPE
MODEL 1901 (London Frequency)
MODEL 2901 (Midlands Frequency)
£336.2.2
(INCLUDING PURCHASE TAX)

476

"His Master's Voice"

477

The RECORD of the MONTH

For EVERY HOME
HIS MASTERS VOICE

479

GIGLI
THE WORLD'S GREATEST TENOR

"HIS MASTER'S VOICE"
Records

478

Greatest Artists
- Finest Recording
"HIS MASTER'S VOICE"

480

SAFE IN MY HEART
(FOX TROT)

MAURICE WINNICK
AND HIS ORCHESTRA

481

IT'S MOST INTERESTING AND INFORMATIVE —
Take a copy home with you

HIS MASTER'S VOICE
RECORD REVIEW

Price 1d.
Monthly

"HIS MASTER'S VOICE"
RECORD REVIEW

482

483

Just Out!

HIS MASTER'S VOICE

"HIS MASTER'S VOICE"

484

A FAVOURITE WITH THE FORCES

REMEMBER SEPTEMBER
(FOX-TROT)
JOE LOSS
AND HIS ORCHESTRA

Transfers and Window Transparencies

We have decided to include this short chapter despite the fact that the collector is very unlikely to find many unused transfers or transparencies and those that were used, either onto windows or doors, or onto delivery vans or lorries would no longer be available in their original state.

It is their very transitory nature, in fact, that makes it difficult to give detailed information on them.

Although the earliest transfer we have traced dates from 1918, it is clear that earlier designs had been available.

Illustration number 485 shows a Victor transfer of 1918, measuring 20½ inches × 14½ inches which was sold to Dealers for 18 cents each.

The 1918 Victor transfer continued to be available through 1921; it was joined in 1919 by a smaller transfer (illus no. 487) which measured 10 inches × 13½ inches. It was lithographed in colours on a white background.

In 1920 the design of the small transfer was changed (illus no. 488), the size remained the same.

In 1919 The Gramophone Company offered its Dealers a Trademark Transfer (illus no. 486). This was reproduced in full colours and measured 14½ inches across the length of the oval.

The Gramophone Company produced a series of Trademark Transfers and Transparencies during the 1930's.

Illustration number 489 shows the small transfer (13 inches × 8¾ inches) and illustration number 490 the large transfer (23 inches × 15½ inches) issued in 1934. 1935 saw the introduction of a Window Transparency Trademark (illus no. 495) printed in colours on bright yellow (11 inches × 8 inches) and a Trademark Transfer also in full colours (illus no. 494) this was in two sizes 23 inches × 17 inches and 15 inches × 11 inches.

In 1936 a new transparency (illus no. 491) measuring 11 inches × 8 inches was produced.

Many of the items mentioned above ran through a number of years, the dates given appear to be the earliest time they were available.

After the War, in 1947 illustration number 492 was issued, printed in colours (15 inches × 10¾ inches).

The following year a new Trademark Window Transparency was released (illus no. 493) measuring 15 inches × 10¾ inches and a Trademark transfer of similar design. It was supplied in three sizes — 10 inches × 7½ inches, 15 inches × 11 inches and 23 inches × 17 inches.

The most recent transfer we have found is shown in illustration number 496. It dates from 1956.

485

HIS MASTER'S VOICE
REG. U.S. PAT. OFF.

487

486

488

489

"His Master's Voice"

490

THE SYMBOL OF SUPREMACY

491

"His Master's Voice" RADIO

493

"His Master's Voice"

492

"HIS MASTER'S VOICE" Sales & Service

494

His Master's Voice

496

"HIS MASTER'S VOICE"

495

"His Master's Voice" RADIO

Cinema Advertising Slides

Up until the War in 1939 and even well beyond that date many cinemas still used glass slides for local advertising purposes.

Both the Victor and Gramophone Companies had a virtually free service supplying their Dealers with suitable advertising slides. These can be very attractive collectable items.

The earliest we have found are Victor slides dating from February 1912. These sold to Dealers at 55 cents each (illus no. 497). Writing to Dealers of this issue the Victor Company stated 'people who patronize the many picture shows are undoubtedly a class to whom the Victor, particularly the popular price Victrolas will make a strong appeal ... Arrange to have them (the slides) shown nightly at the many picture parlours. You will impress the Victor idea on many people you can reach in no other way'. A second set (illus no. 498) was issued in April 1912 still at 55 cents each.

In October 1913 Victor produced a new set of twelve Christmas slides (illus no. 499) at the same time reducing the price to 25 cents each.

Some of the slides from 1918 reflect the War (illus no. 500) whilst the post War series of 1924 took on a more modern look (illus no. 501).

The Gramophone Company too produced a Slide Service. Illustration numbers 504-505 show two from 1924; illustration number 506 shows a slide from 1927. Illustration number 503 is from 1934 and illustration number 502 from 1938, whilst numbers 507-509 date from 1941. Late Wartime and immediate Post War periods are reflected in illustration numbers 510-515.

The series then available was free of charge to Dealers. It also included slides featuring every radio and television in the current H.M.V. range as well as gramophones and records.

The provision of glass slides was discontinued as more and more cinemas went over to film strip advertising. A selection of more interesting slides will be admired by fellow collectors of 'Nipperie'.

260

264

268

261

265

269

262

266

270

263

267

271

501

502

503

504

505

506

507

508

509

510

511

512

513

514

515

Travel and Transport

'Nipper' Car Badges and 'His Master's Voice' Car Number Plates

In July 1935 The Gramophone Company announced to its Dealers, 'After the production of several different designs of car badges, we have selected one which we believe equals, if not surpasses, the finest badge that ever adorned a car'.

The Trademark was produced in relief, in such detail that even the stylus bar and needle of the sound box are clearly visible. The lettering 'His Master's Voice' was enamelled in red. The badge was given a semi-dull finish and was supplied with a right angle bracket fitting (illus no. 516). It was sold to Dealers and their staffs at a charge of 6/- (30p) and continued to be available at this price until the War in 1939.

In 1937 through the good offices of the Middlesex County Council The Gramophone Company were able to make arrangements for a block of 'HMV' car index numbers to be allocated to the Company for its own cars and the cars of its staff members and Dealers living in the Middlesex area. Dealers living in the area could arrange for their cars to have 'HMV' numbers by writing to the Traffic Manager of the Company (illus no. 517). It was stated that the 'HMV' index numbers could not be allocated to commercial vehicles, neither could they be taken up by Dealers living outside the Middlesex area who did not purchase their cars through a Middlesex distributor. If the new 'HMV' index number was to be applied to a previously registered vehicle, then a £5 fee was payable to the Registration Authorities for each transfer. An 'HMV' index registration number plate may well be an interesting acquisition for a collector.

In Canada where car registration policy is much more liberal than in Britain, the outstanding 'Nipper' collector Diamond 'Jim' Greer obtained a personalized license plate for his classic 1963 Cadillac. His plate, well what else but 'NIPPER' (illus no. 519).

Delivery Lorries and Vans

Although subject to repainting and, of course, obsolescence, we thought it of interest to show some of the outstanding 'Nipper' orientated delivery lorries and vans.

In 1917 the Victor Talking Machine Company of Philadelphia was using a delivery van of intriguing design. The rear body was built in the shape of a two console Victrola. 'Nipper' sat firmly on the top of the driving cab (illus no. 520).

Also in 1917 The Knight-Campbell Music Company used the same idea for their motor cycle and side car delivery unit (illus no. 521).

Illustration number 518 dates from January 1920 and shows the delivery van of A.B. Clinton Company of Hertford, Conn. The wheels were imitations of Victor Red Seal Records, complete with label numbers, title and artist. Note 'Nipper' on the bonnet.

517

516

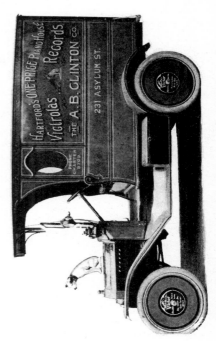

518

During the same year a magnificently appointed delivery van (illus no. 522) was in use by L. Meier and Sons of Cleveland, Ohio. Again the idea of turning the rear body into a Victrola has been adopted.

During the late 1920's The Gramophone Company had a fine fleet of delivery vehicles in use. Illustration number 523 shows part of this fleet preparing for its morning departure from Blyth Road, outside part of the Hayes factory complex.

Two other lorries from the fleet are shown in illustrations numbers 524-525.

Perhaps, tucked away in an old garage or barn, some of these grand old vehicles may still be alive under a coating of grime and dust.

Of course, individual Dealers both in Britain and in the U.S.A. would all have had their own delivery and service vans. Many of these may well have features to interest the 'Nipper' enthusiast.

A footnote comes from Mort Gaffin of RCA, who announced that starting on October 31st 1978 as part of the general reintroduction of 'Nipper' on the Company's products, "he'll even get a free ride on the side of RCA Service Company trucks". So, once again 'Nipper' will be seen proudly appearing on lorries and vans, in the U.S.A. at any rate!

Trains

The railway too, was not forgotten. In 1934 The Gramophone Company launched its H.M.V. National Show Train to promote the Company's products. Two large scenery waggons and one restaurant car were adapted by covering the outside faces of the vans with a new thin shell and decorating them as in illustration number 526.

On April 27th 1934 Prime Minister Ramsay MacDonald gave the train a ceremonial send-off on its nationwide journey. From April 27th to August 2nd the train travelled 3,000 miles and was visited by 145,834 people including ten Lord Mayors and 43 Mayors.

Those readers whose experience of railway travel goes back to the pre-war days of the 1930's may remember seeing the station name board at Hayes and Harlington (illus no. 527) which proudly proclaimed the town as being 'The Home of His Master's Voice'. What happened to this famous sign? Did it end up in some railway enthusiast's collection etc?

Delivery Packaging

It seems unlikely that many collectors will want to acquire a whole collection of delivery crates and cartons or other delivery packing. However, we feel that this subject should receive a brief mention and this appears to be the most appropriate place into which to squeeze it.

Illustration numbers 528-529 show the wooden delivery crates used by the Victor Company in 1921. The Gramophone Company tended to make greater use of less durable cardboard cartons.

From around 1936 to the outbreak of the War in 1939 The Gramophone Company issued Felt Padded Transport Covers, designed for the short trip movement of large radio gramophones (illus no. 530). This was sold to Dealers at a price of 35/- (£1.75) each.

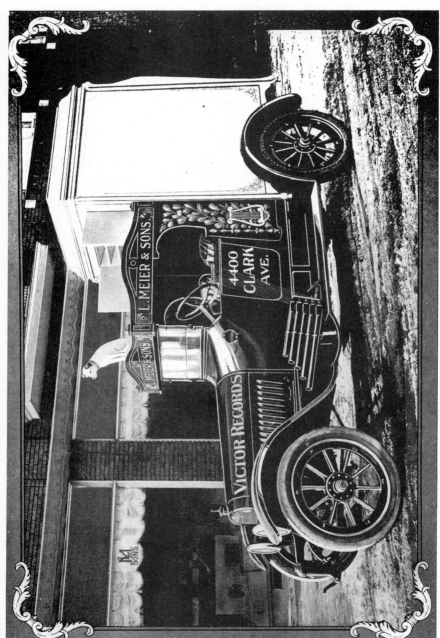

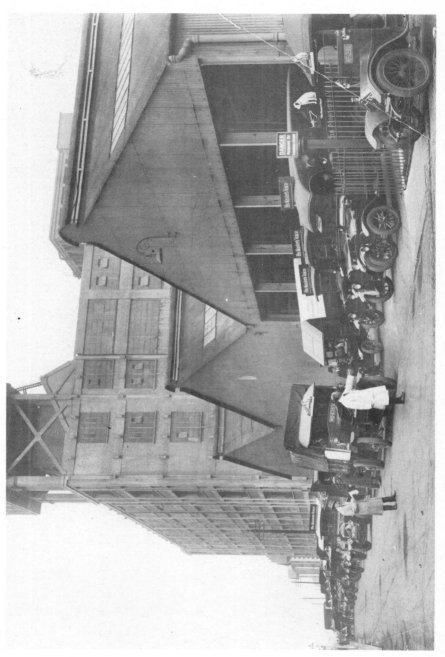

526

527

530

529

528

Buildings with 'Nipper' Associations

Certain buildings have a special association with 'Nipper' and display or once displayed 'Nipper' symbols on their roofs or facades.

We feel that a brief note should be made of some of those known to us. Obviously you can't collect them, although you can go and see them if you happen to be in their locality.

EMI Records have, long since, left their historic old site at Blyth Road, Hayes in Middlesex. The well known old HQ Building is no longer occupied by the Company and 'Nipper' no longer swings round on his weather vane looking out over the country which he has lorded over for the past 73 years. This famous sign has now been taken down. It is hoped that it will pass into the keeping of the EMI Music Archives, now situated at 1-3 Uxbridge Road, Hayes, where it will be re-erected on the EMI Record Factory at that site.

By August 1911 a Mr Blomfield had been asked to prepare drawings for an 'His Master's Voice' weather vane to stand on top of the clock turret of The Gramophone Company's Headquarters at Hayes in Middlesex. By August 22nd 1911 Mr Blomfield had reported that the cost of the vane would be £15.00. He was instructed to proceed with the vane and also the installation of the clock, both of which were in place by late 1911 or early 1912.

Illustration number 531 shows the 'Nipper' weather vane still in place during 1980.

Another famous landmark, which was located in Camden, N.J., U.S.A. has also disappeared. In 1915 four stained glass windows, each measuring 14½ feet in diameter, were installed in the tower of the Victor Talking Machine Company's building at Camden. These were lighted at night and could be clearly seen in Philadelphia. They were a landmark along the Delaware River waterfront for some fifty-four years.

These windows were designed by Nicola D'Ascenzo in 1915. They were to be installed in the top of the tower of the Cabinet Factory which was completed and employing some 6,000 workers by 1917. They remained in place until April 1969 when, due to changes of marketing policy they were removed and the spaces covered with white boards carrying the RCA logo. One of these windows is with the Smithsonian Institute in Washington D.C.; two others are with the Widner College, Chester and Penn State, University Park, Pa. Happily one is still retained by RCA.

A splendid ending to the story was repeated by Steven I. Ramm in 'The Hillandale News' of June 1979. With the advent of Edgar H. Griffiths as the new President of RCA in 1976, plans were made to reinstate 'Nipper'. It was decided to replace the historic windows and new ones were ordered from the original manufacturers. The new windows were dedicated ten years to the day that the former ones were removed. A crowd of about 500 people, mostly RCA employees and their families gathered to see the new windows being lighted

HAYES   JULY `80.

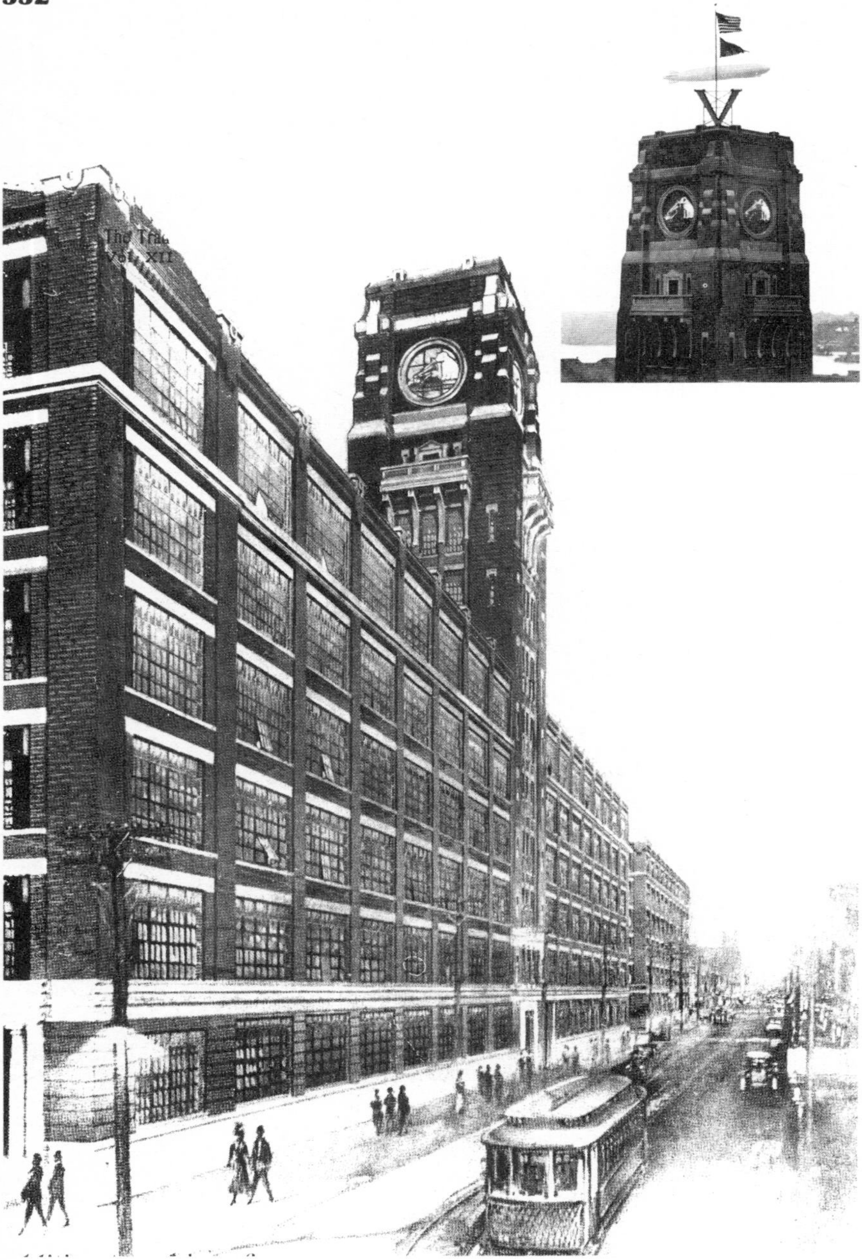

and the Governor of New Jersey declared April 10th 1979 'Nipper Day'.

Illustration number 532 shows two of the windows in place soon after the opening of the Cabinet Factory in 1917. The insert shows the Graf Zeppelin sailing past the tower and the windows, in 1928.

Whilst on a visit to the RCA Headquarters one of the authors photographed a small stained glass window in the President's Suite (illus no. 537). We know nothing of the history of this piece.

Mention has been made of 'The World's Largest Nipper' in the section 'Models of Nipper', however, we feel that this four ton replica must claim attention here too. Illustration number 533 shows the 25½ foot high Dog in his place on top of 911 Broadway, Albany, the HQ of the RTA Corporation, an RCA Distributor. He is one of the tourist attractions of the town.

Britain's Giant 'Nipper' is also mentioned in 'Models of Nipper'. This 4 foot 6 inch high model Dog and his Gramophone is now displayed over the entrance of EMI Records Production and Distribution Building, 1-3 Uxbridge Road, Hayes.

Pedestrians passing past the EMI Uxbridge Road complex can peer over the hedge and catch a glimpse of the 'giant'.

Most record collectors worth their name will have at least heard of the 'His Master's Voice' Record Store in Oxford Street, London. This famous shop was opened by Sir Edward Elgar on July 20th 1921. All went happily along until the night of December 26th 1937 when the store was gutted by a disastrous fire which also claimed the life of the solitary night watchman who was on duty at that time.

Illustration number 534 was taken on December 28th 1937. Amidst the devastation 'Nipper' still stands supreme and virtually untouched, surely a symbol of the durability of this famous Dog and his Gramophone.

Illustration number 535 shows the rebuilt store facade as it appeared on Coronation Day 1953.

To mark the 75th anniversary of The Gramophone Company, Ind Coope Limited dedicated a West End Public House to the memory of 'Nipper'. On that day the old 'Marlborough Head' in Great Marlborough Street, London received a new name, 'The Dog and Trumpet' — its inn sign being a replica of the original painting by Francis Barraud (illus no. 536). In cooperation with EMI the pub has been embellished with a collection of historical items, including a Thompson copy of the 'His Master's Voice' painting and an original Trademark Gramophone and plaster 'Nipper'.

535

This magnificent Coronation
Day Picture was taken as
Her Majesty the Queen and
the Duke of Edinburgh passed
our Oxford Street Show-
rooms on their return journey
to Buckingham Palace.

*A copy of this photograph is available free
of charge to "His Master's Voice" dealers,
upon application to Advertising Division,
E.M.I. Sales & Service Ltd., Hayes,
Middx.*

537

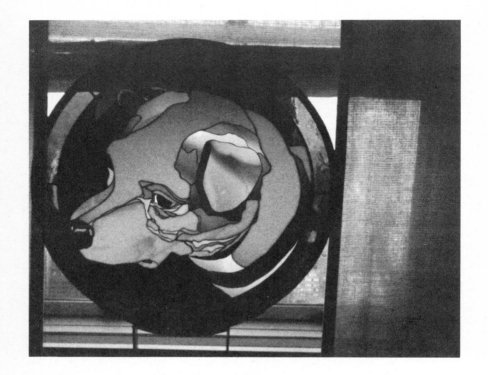

Games and Pastimes

Jig Saw Puzzles

Both the Gramophone and Victor Companies have produced some very collectable 'Nipper' puzzles over the years. In 1911 The Gramophone Company had twelve wooden puzzles prepared carrying a photographic reproduction of the Dog picture. These were sent out to the British and Overseas Branches to test reaction as a promotional sales aid. It is not known whether these ever went into mass production.

During 1913 preparations seem to have been made to produce a jig saw puzzle of 'His Master's Voice In 50 Languages'. Again it is not known if these puzzles were produced.

In 1922 the Victor Company entered the puzzle field claiming to be the first national advertiser to use jig saw puzzles to advertise in this way.

Illustrations numbers 539-541 show two puzzles issued at this time, each puzzle being packed in an envelope which encourages the customer to do the puzzle over and over again. He was urged to 'try for a speed record'. The company announced that "Persons in the Victor companies' offices who never saw the puzzles before they were placed before them took anywhere from half to a quarter of an hour to put these together", although it was rather smugly stated that 'one departmental head attained a record of two minutes and forty-three seconds'.

These puzzles were sold to Dealers at $15 per 1,000 with a suggestion that they be given away to customers 'just hand the envelope out saying nothing about it. To explain is to take the fun out of opening the envelope'. At this price the puzzles would have cost around 1½ cents each!!

Later designs of Victor jig saw puzzles were packed in boxes representing a Victor orthophonic gramophone.

In 1928 The Gramophone Company spurred on by the success of jig saw puzzles issued by the Great Western Railway, produced 5,000 puzzles of the Trademark Picture. These were sold to Dealers at 8/- (40p) per dozen. The Dealer in turn re-selling the puzzles to his customers at 1/- (5p) each.

Games and Competitions

During 1900 The Gramophone Company experimented in producing a few special 7 inch multi track Puzzle Records. These usually consisted of three selections — a song, a band piece and an instrumental selection. They were recorded in parallel, the selection played depended upon the point of the circumference on which the needle was placed.

In order to promote these records and also to create publicity for the infant gramophone, in the Autumn of 1900 Barry Owen, the Managing Director of The Gramophone Company Ltd. extensively advertised a competition consisting of a scrambled picture (illus no. 544) which had to be rearranged to reveal a

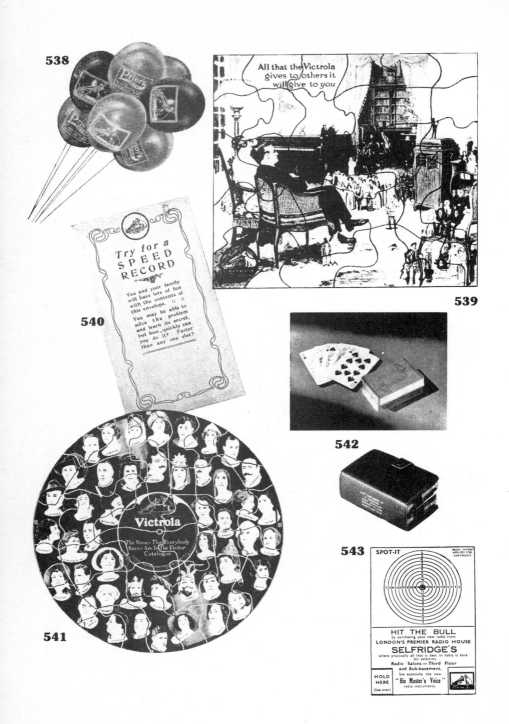

538

539
All that the Victrola gives to others it will give to you

540
Try for a SPEED RECORD

You and your family will have lots of fun with the contents of this envelope. :: :: You may be able to solve the problem and learn its secret, but how quickly can you do it? Faster than any one else?

541
Victrola
The Names That Everybody Knows Are In The Victor Catalogue

542

543

544

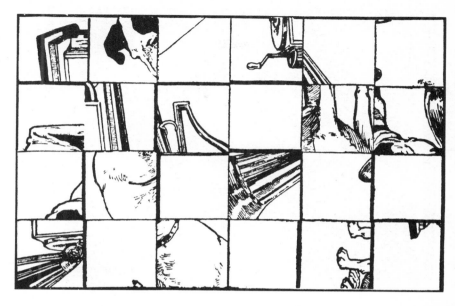

545

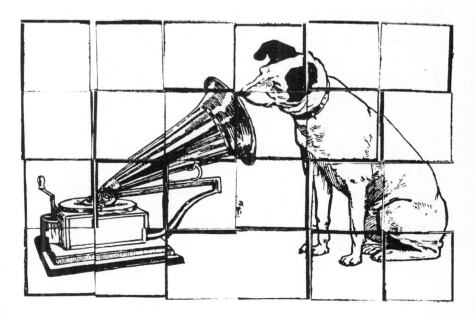

546

547

548

Neujahrs-Bilderrätsel.

Lösung des Neujahrs-Bilderrätsels aus No. 1:

Getrost dem neuen Jahr entgegen
Geh'n wir geschlossen im Verein.
Und was es bringt an Glück und Segen
Soll für die ganze Menschheit sein.

549

Neujahrsrätsel.

550

Neujahrsrätsel:
Viel Glück im neuen Jahre.

Liest man diese Buchstaben in der richtigen Reihenfolge ab, dann ergiebt sich ein sehr bekannter Ausspruch Kaiser Wilhelm II.

Bilder-Rätsel:
Alleweg guet Zohre!

551

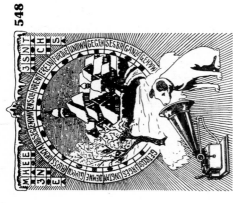

Fasching-Rätsel.

Die Lösung des „Fasching-Rätsels" aus No. 2 unserer Zeitschrift lautet:
Im Februar geht's auf jeden Fall
Auf den hochlustigen Maskenball;
Da wird charmiert, getanzt, gelacht,
Und mancher Ulk dabei gemacht.

representation of an already famous painting (illus no. 545). The successful result had to be pasted on a sheet of paper and sent to The Gramophone Company who would present to the successful contestants one of the new puzzle records as a prize.

In 1911 the German Branch of The Gramophone Company put out their version of the Nipper Puzzle (illus nos. 546-547). In this case however no prize appears to have been offered for solving the problem.

During 1912/14 the German Branch began to include a series of jumbled slogans and poems in its monthly magazine 'Die Stimme seines Herrn'. The reader had to rearrange the fragments of words to form a sentence or even a complete poem. A number of these puzzles featured Nipper and these have been reproduced in illustrations numbers 548 to 551. For our reader's ease of mind the solution is given under each puzzle.

In June 1912 the Victor Company released a very clever advertising puzzle book for Victor Dealers entitled 'Musical Mysteries' which was issued by the Pictorial Publishing Company of New York. It contained twelve pages, ten of which had pictorial puzzles or enigmas all centering on the merits of Victor Gramophones. The remaining two pages as well as the cover were devoted to advertising.

The Victor Company's game of 'Red Seal Derby' consisted of a cardboard race track (illus no. 552). It was manufactured and distributed by C.C. Mellar Company of Pittsburgh, Pa. in 1921.

It seems to have been devised for Dealers Sales Staff as an aid to increase their knowledge of Victor Records. The names of Victor Red Seal artists were 'posted' all around the track and the score was kept of the number of records sold of each artist during the period of the Derby. The rules ominously noted 'if any sales fail to appear against the "record" of any individual artists, that means that the sales staff doesn't know the catalogue, for all good Victor students know the records of every Red Seal artist can be sold'.

Each member of sales staff was assigned a colour and his score in the Derby marked up under that colour. However, before anyone was allowed to begin to run in the race he had to sell at least $500 of records to get to the start. The first salesman to clock up $500 of Red Seal sales won the race and a new Derby was started.

The Victor Mystic Oracle (illus no. 556) was supplied to Victor Dealers by the Reincke-Ellis Company of Chicago.

It consisted of a four page folder. On page three was a moveable dial with a series of questions about the Victrola printed on. The enquiring salesman turned the dial until one of the questions came under the arrow printed on the page. He then closed the folder and on the front cover he would find a metal arrow pointing to the answer. Page two gave a number of 'interesting and not generally known facts about the Victrola', whilst the back page listed some 'appealing Victor records'. The Mystic oracle which was available during 1925 was advertised as 'a unique sales device and a delightful game for children and grown ups and, whether they wish it or not, some pretty strong Victor sales talk and some interesting questions and answers are impressed upon them. It is as amusing as a crossword puzzle and much more effective since it answers in straightforward language most of the ordinary questions and some of the extra-ordinary ones that are asked about the Victrola and Victor records'.

Another sales aid was invented by Miss Alice Keith of the Victor Company

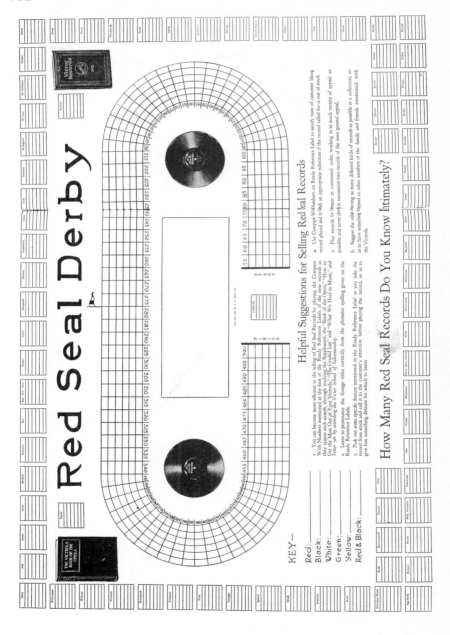

Red Seal Derby

KEY—

Red: _____
Black: _____
White: _____
Green: _____
Yellow: _____
Red & Black: _____

Helpful Suggestions for Selling Red Seal Records

1. You can become more efficient in the selling of Red Seal Records by playing the Compare With Numbers mentioned at the foot of the Ready Reference Labels of the new records as they appear each month, through studying the Supplement, the "Book of the Opera," "How to Get the Most Out of Your Victrola," "The Graded List" and "What We Hear in Music," and better yet by attending the *Victor School of Salesmanship*.

2. Learn to pronounce the foreign titles correctly from the phonetic spelling given on the Ready Reference Labels.

3. Pick out some specific feature mentioned on the Ready Reference Label as you take the record from stock and call it to the customer's attention before playing the record, so as to give him something definite for which to listen.

4. Use Compare With Numbers on Ready Reference Label to satisfy taste of customer liking record played and to finish an appropriate substitute if the record called for is out of stock.

5. Play records for customer in contrasted order, working in as much variety of appeal as possible and never play in succession two records of the same general appeal.

6. Suggest the value of having as many different kinds of records as possible in a collection, so as to have something to appeal to older members of the family and friends entertained with the Victrola.

How Many Red Seal Records Do You Know Intimately?

553

556

554

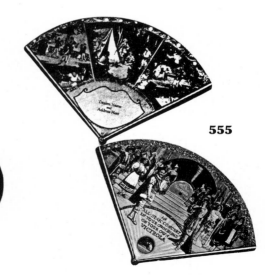

555

HORIZONTAL

1. Vertical line between measures.
2. A song about this brew is sung by Plunkett in Opera "Martha."
3. First syllable in old scale adopted from "Hymn to John the Baptist."
4. Sixth tone of the major scale flatted.
5. Tempo at which Victor goods should be purchased (slang).
6. Class to which Victor products belong.
7. First name of great Welsh American Tenor who died in 1918.
8. Spanish Tenor who did not sing in third Victor Radio-Concert.
9. Initials of famous woman pianist.
10. Many songs about this are written for bass singers.
11. Short for "all Victor."
12. United-States musical capital (abbr.).
13. A mythical "König" about whom Franz Schubert wrote a song.
14. Composer of "Orientale."
15. A person who should possess a Victrola.
16. A domestic animal made famous through a trade mark.
17. The first word in "Brünnhilde's Battle Cry" from the Opera "Walküre."
18. First word in a famous song by Kipling (Mandalay)
19. The third tone of the major scale flatted.

VERTICAL

1. The original "pastoral symphony."
6. A latin prayer sung in Roman Catholic Churches. (One famous one by Bach-Gounod).
7. A character in the Opera "Lohengrin."
8. Something no Victor product has.
13. A coloratura song sung by Galli-Curci.
17. Name of an American contralto of fame.
20. A famous "Red Seal" artist born in Holland.
21. The first name of a director of a jazz orchestra.
22. Something no member of an orchestra should lose. (Letter instead of word).
23. A famous prima donna, who sang in second Victor Radio-Concert.
24. Second tone of the major scale.
25. First two words in title of a composition by Macdowell.
26. A great U. S. organization whose band in Washington, D. C., is directed by Santelmann.
27. A fox trot played by Whiteman's Orchestra.
28. A very popular woman song writer.
29. A vocal composition.
30. Speaking of Victrolas, every home should have at least this many.

SOLUTION

HORIZONTAL

1. bar
2. ale
3. ut
4. le
5. P. D. Q.
6. A
7. Evan
8. Fleta
9. O. S. (Olga Samaroff)
10. sea
11. A. V. (all Victor)
12. N. Y.
13. Erl
14. Cui
15. I
16. dog
17. Ho
18. On
19. Me

VERTICAL

1. Ba! (of a sheep)
6. Ave
7. Elsa
8. foe
13. Echo
17. Homer
20. Culp
21. Ted (Weems)
22. Q
23. Alda
24. Re
25. At An (Old Trysting Place)
26. Navy
27. Eliza
28. Bond (Carrie Jacobs)
29. song
30. one

Travelling Staff in 1925. A 'Nipper' Dog crossword puzzle (illus no. 557).   Note
the black squares spell out 'VTM' (Victor Talking Machine).

During 1917 the Victor Company produced a 'Ten Good Victor Records' fan
(illus no. 553). Three years later Victor issued the 'Victor Record Fan' (illus no.
554). It was 8½ inches in diameter and with wooden handles 8½ inches long.
Dealers were charged $10 for 250 fans. The following year a Victrola fan was
produced by the Reincke-Ellis Company of New York City (illus no. 555). 250
fans cost the Dealer $10.75. We assume these fans were intended for Dance and
party use, however, we suppose they could always be used if you became too
hot and bothered constructing jig saw puzzles in record time!

Almost from the beginning the Victor and Gramophone Companies produced
'Nipper' playing cards.

In 1902 The Gramophone Company made enquiries of the American Card
Playing Company of Cincinnati (the manufacturers of Bicycle cards) asking for
a quotation for 100,000-250,000 sets of playing cards with reproductions of the
H.M.V. painting on the backs. We have not traced whether these cards actually
went into production at that time.

In the mid 1930's The Gramophone Company produced sets of playing cards
with the H.M.V. Trademark printed in gold on crimson or blue on the back of
each card (illus no. 542). These were sold to Dealers for 2/- (10p) for two packs.
Leatherette cases to hold two packs with Dealer's name and address in gold
blocking were available at 8/- (40p) per dozen. In September 1936 it was
announced that the card cases would be available made of real morocco leather
at no additional cost. However, by 1938 the set was again advertised in
leatherette cases.

Balloons, for parties, are always popular. A series, in a variety of colours,
bearing the H.M.V. Trademark and the Dealer's name and address were
available throughout most of the 1930's at 7/6d per gross (37½p) (illus no. 538).

In March 1936 The Gramophone Company issued 'Spot It' Cards (illus no.
543). We have not seen any of these and as the instructions for playing the
game are printed on the reverse of the card, which is not shown, we can tell the
reader nothing more about them except that they were available to Dealers at a
cost of 12/6d (62½p) per 100.

Books Published Under
the 'Nipper' Imprint

Both the Victor and Gramophone Companies have, over the years, been prolific publishers. Between them they have probably issued hundreds of thousands of leaflets and thousands of books, all bearing the 'Nipper' imprint.

Naturally the Main Record Catalogues and the Monthly Supplement Lists are amongst the most important publications to come from these Houses. Any Record Catalogues that come your way should be preserved. Even the most modern will become the collector's pieces of the future. Any Catalogues dating prior to 1930 are already quite scarce and those prior to 1910 are very rare indeed. In 1950 E.M.I. began to publish large cloth bound Record Catalogues listing all its Marks. Unlike earlier catalogues, these were not available to the public, being intended only for Trade use; only some 3,000-5,000 copies of each edition being printed, depending upon the year. These are already quite scarce and will certainly become collector's prizes in a few years time. Remember, also, that both Companies produced Catalogues and Supplements for all the different countries in which they traded. Some examples of The Gramophone Company's lists from India and the Middle East are very exotic and are attractive to the collector, even though printed in the vernacular.

The companion to the Main Record Catalogue is the Numerical Catalogue, which, as its name implies, lists all the Company's records in *numerical* order. These were issued only to the Trade and are always much sort after by collectors.

Monthly Record Supplements are generally much rarer than the same year's Main Catalogues. Because the latter were books, people tended to place them on their book shelves and preserve them, whereas the ephemeral nature of the Monthly List encouraged disposal after reading. Never neglect to collect any Monthly Record Supplements you may find, they are both interesting and valuable to the collector.

In addition to the Main Record Catalogue, other special listings were issued, the most important for the collector being the Instrument (Gramophone) Catalogues, issued annually or sometimes twice yearly. A collection of these is a very desirable acquisition and an invaluable guide to the original price, date of issue and length of availability of the Company's instruments.

Apart from the catalogues, perhaps the most well known publications from both Companies are The Victrola/Victor Book of the Opera and Opera at Home, telling the story of the operas and linking them to Victor and H.M.V. records. Both publications went into many editions, all of which are very collectable. A word of warning, the first edition of The Gramophone Company's Opera at Home issued in 1920, was a paperback and not in the well known hardback cloth bound format which first came out a year later. The first edition of The Victrola Book of the Opera appeared in 1912.

Numerous special Company promotional booklets were issued over the years,

558

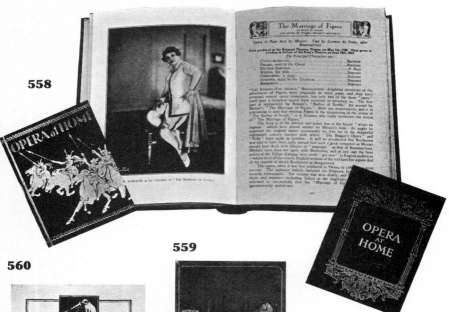

559

560

561

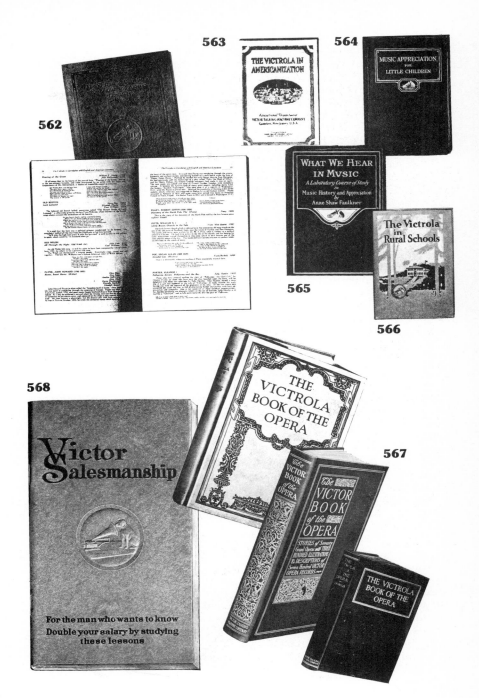

562

563

564

565

566

567

568

including:
The Living Voice circa 1906
The Home of the Gramophone February 1920 (reprinted in 1924 for Wembley
                    Exhibition)
The Romance of Victor
The Home of the Gramophone 1929 (not as good as the 1920 edition)
Writing in Sound — How a Gramophone Record is made 1938
The Pursuit of High Fidelity 1955 and 1961
Once Upon a Record (1961)
Making Records at EMI (1968)
Play Back (1977)

During 1911 the Victor Company formed its Public School Educational Department, later to be known merely as Educational Department. Although it had produced a number of records of educational value, it was not until 1919 that The Gramophone Company followed Victor's example and formed their official Educational Department. These Divisions of the two Companies produced some of the most important publications issued by them and form some valuable source material on the early use of the Gramophone in education.

Neither Company appears to have retained a detailed listing of all the publications issued by them, and we of course, can only comment upon those items that we have seen. Certainly, any books or booklets issued by the Educational Department of the two Companies should be retained by the collector, for this reason we list below some of the more important items we have noted.

	Date of First
Victor Educational Publications	*Known Edition*
Special Records for School & Home Use	1911
Graded List of Records of Practical School Use	1911
The Victor on the Playground	1912
What we hear in Music (went into many editions)	1913
A Graded List of Victor Records for Children in School and Home (went into many editions)	1913
The Victor in Commercial Studies (typewriting, penmanship & stenography)	1915
The Victor in Schools — correlates music with the entire curriculum	1915
The Victrola in Rural Schools (numerous editions)	1916
New Victor Records for Educational Use	1917
The Victrola in Physical Education, Recreation & Play	1917
The Victor in Americanization	—
Instruments of the Orchestra (many editions)	1918
A New Graded List of Victor Records for Children in Home and School	1918
Outlines of a Brief Study of Music Appreciation for High Schools (a number of editions)	1920
The Victor in Correlation with English & American Literature	1921
Music Appreciation for Little Children	—

569

571

572

16

573

570

574

576

577

575

578

The Victrola in Music Memory Contests	1922
Music and Romance	—
Music Manual for Rural Schools with the Victrola (formerly entitled 'The Victrola in Rural Schools')	1924
Revised Lessons – Music Appreciation with the Victrola for Children	1927
Victor Records for Elementary Schools (this appears to be the 17th edition of 'The Graded List of Victor Records')	1937

The Gramophone Company's Educational Publications	*Publication Date*
A Note on the Employment of the Gramophone in the Teaching of Languages	1906
H.M.V. Records for Teachers and Parents	1919
Appreciation of Music – the place of the Gramophone in Music Education	1920
The Gramophone in School — Catalogue of Educational Records (large number of editions 1920's-1950's)	—
Melody Making — Sir Walford Davies	1923
English Poetry Records — Plum Label	1929
A Chart book of English Literature, History & Music — Cyril Winn	1924
How to use the Gramophone in Schools:	
1. Listening to Music — Alec Robertson & Peter Latham	—
2. Why and When — Alec Robertson & Peter Latham	
3. Picture and Story Music — Alec Robertson & Peter Latham	—
4. Schubert — Alec Robertson & Peter Latham	—
5. The Rhythmic Road to Music Land — Hilda Habbershaw	—
Playways – Records for Young Children — Mrs J Murray Macbain	—
The Golden Treasury of Recorded Music — Alec Robertson:	
1. Bach and Beethoven	1928
2. Wagner	1929
3. Cesar Franck	—
4. Johannes Brahms	—
The Student of Singing & the Gramophone — Dawson Freer	—
Handbook of Language Records	—
Folk Dance Records	—
Maypole Dancing to H.M.V.	—
Physical Culture Exercises on H.M.V. Records	1923
Music for Movement	1951
Catalogue of Mood Music (2nd edition 1938)	1937
Instruments of the orchestra (numerous editions)	—
Learning to Listen by means of the Gramophone — Percy A Scholes	1921
Record Collector's Series — Norman Demuth:	
1. Forming a basic Library	1949
2. Symphonies	1950
3. Concertos	1950

In addition, both Companies issued special text books to accompany their various language courses — French, German, Russian, Italian, Spanish, etc.

The reader's attention is also drawn to a superb 365 page book on the use of

Das Grammophon
im Dienſte des Unterrichts und der Wiſſenſchaft

von

Oberlehrer Dᴿ Otto Drieſen, Charlottenburg

Band I, Teil 1:
Kindergarten, Volksſchule, Mittelſchule, Höhere Lehranſtalten

Band I, Teil 2:
Textproben für Kindergarten, Volksſchule, Mittelſchule, Höhere Lehranſtalten

Band II: Univerſitäten (in Vorbereitung)

Berlin 1913
Verlag der Deutſchen Grammophon-Aktiengeſellſchaft, Berlin S.42, Ritterſtraße 35.

579

Das Grammophon
im Dienſte des Unterrichts und der Wiſſenſchaft
(Sammlung Dᴿ Drieſen)

Syſtematiſche Sammlung von Grammophonplatten
für den Unterricht
vom Kindergarten bis zur Univerſität

Entworfen,
zur techniſchen Aufnahme durchgeführt unter Heranziehung beſonders geeigneter Vortragenden
und mit einem Vorwort über die grammophoniſche Unterrichtsmethode nebſt Textproben
herausgegeben von
Oberlehrer Dᴿ Otto Drieſen, Charlottenburg

Band I, Teil 1:
(Kindergarten, Volksſchule, Mittelſchule, Höhere Lehranſtalten)

Berlin 1913
Verlag der Deutſchen Grammophon-Aktiengeſellſchaft, Berlin S.42.

the Gramophone in Education, produced by The Gramophone Company's German Branch in 1913. It is filled with information and pictures and would surely be a great find for a collector. The title pages of this volume are reproduced in illustration number 579.

Both the Victor and Gramophone Companies issued a House Magazine for distribution within the Company and to its Dealers. The Victor publication was entitled 'The Voice of Victor' whilst The Gramophone Company contented itself with 'The Voice'. Other Branch Companies of The Gramophone Company had their own House Magazines, all of which are of interest and well worth preserving if any came your way.

Illustrations numbers 558-579, show a selection of the publications mentioned in this chapter.

Paper Record Covers and Delivery Envelopes

Always keep any paper record covers which bear the H.M.V. Trademark. They will form an attractive addition to your collection. The series issued by The Gramophone Company in the 1930's, many featuring artists listening to various models of H.M.V. gramophones, are often of interest. Illustration number 586 shows a selection of designs. Note Yvonne Printemps with her 'Nipper Look-Alike' dog.

During the 1920's the Victor Company introduced 'Record Delivery Envelopes' which were in fact really high class bags into which the Dealer put the customer's records after purchase (illus nos. 580 and 585).

They were supplied to Dealers in two sizes — 11½ inches and 13½ inches. Not only were these envelopes attractive and useful in themselves, they also had other work to do as the Victor Company explained to its Dealers:

"if you sell a customer one or more dance records almost automatically you are tempted to place his purchase in a Victor delivery envelope showing the dancing couple and calling attention to the fact that 'the best dance music will be found on Victor Records'. He has just bought some and he is tolerably well sold on the fact that Victor music is the best dance music. The better way is to place his dance records in the envelope showing 'The Love Duet from Faust' and containing the message 'All the great music of opera by the greatest Victor artists is available on Victor Records'. If he is a consistent purchaser of Victor dance music always put his purchases into the opera envelope, thus you will plant a new thought — and a new desire. The reverse works out equally well — an operatic record customer can usually be influenced to add a few dance numbers to his periodic purchases. The right envelope consistently used to put over the Victrola instrument idea has sold more than one instrument. If you know that your record purchaser is going to play the records on an instrument not a Victrola, make it your business to sell him one. Place his records in the envelope showing the Victor Trademark or that bearing the Victrola instrument illustration'.

Whilst thinking of record shop bags, collectors are recommended to take a special look at the plastic bag in which their latest record purchase was handed over to them. Some of these have quite an interesting look. The HMV group of Record Shops have produced some good 'Nipper' designs. He recently appeared on a black and white leopard skin background!

A small collection of these envelopes together with interesting Dealer's record bags could form an attractive addition to your 'Nipperie'.

580

from

YOUR NAME AND ADDRESS
WILL BE PRINTED HERE

for

581

"HIS MASTER'S VOICE"

Both the picture "His Master's Voice" and the word Victrola are exclusive trademarks of the Victor Talking Machine Company. When you see these trademarks on a sound reproducing instrument or record you can be sure it was made by the Victor Company

582

Victrola — the instrument specially made to play Victor Records

583

The Best Dance Music
will be found on
Victor Records

584

All the Great Music of Opera by the Greatest Artists is available on Victor Records

585

New Victor Records—
Once a Week. Every Week. Friday

Catalogue, Supplement and Magazine Binders

Over the years both the Victor and Gramophone Companies issued many handsome binder covers to house their publications.

Here we give a small selection as a guide to the variety of cover you may find. Certainly, any cover carrying the Dog is worth keeping if it comes your way, either merely to look at or to actually use on your own catalogues etc.

In 1913 the Victor Company produced a binder for its house magazine 'The Voice of Victor' (illus no. 587) which sold to Dealers at 18 cents.

Much later, in 1926 a revised cover, in imitation leather which held eighteen copies of the magazine, was produced (illus no. 588).

In October 1919 the Victor Company issued a special Catalogue and Supplement Binder (illus no. 589). This was bound in black imitation leather. A de-luxe model was available bound in genuine leather. It was possible for the Dealer to resell these binders to customers.

In May 1921 Victor released an extremely handsome cover to house both the complete Victor Record Catalogue and all record Supplements for a year (illus no. 590). These sold for $1.60, later reduced to $1.40 each. By the end of the year the catalogue cover was supplemented by one for the numerical catalogue (illus no. 591). This was bound in black leather cloth and sold to Dealers for $1.50.

Both the last two items were still available in 1926 and by now the catalogue/supplement binder could be sold to the public, the price to the Dealer now being reduced to 50 cents.

In the early 1920's The Gramophone Company produced a Catalogue and Supplement binder of very similar design to the Victor shown in illustration number 590. It was bound in a rather dull brown cloth, the design being impressed into the cover but not highlighted by any printed colour.

During the 1930's The Gramophone Company issued various covers. Those in illustration number 592 all cost the Dealer 1/6d (7½p) each. In 1936 The Gramophone Company introduced a linen covered binder to contain its own house magazine 'The Voice' (illus no. 594). This was produced in two tones of blue and sold to Dealers for 1/- (5p). In 1938 the design was changed (illus no. 595) and the price increased to 1/3d (6½p).

In 1934 a specially designed auto-radiogram, based upon Model 800 was supplied to HRH The Prince of Wales. The Service Manual accompanying the instrument was given a special cover of leather (illus no. 598). The Service Manuals Binder shown in illustration number 596 bound in imitation Morocco leather was also released in 1934 selling to Dealers for 1/6d (7½p).

The Radio Times cover appeared during 1934/36. It had padded blue leatherette covers which could be stamped with the Dealer's name and address. Inside was the story of the 'His Master's Voice' Trademark and a montage picture of the H.M.V. Factory at Hayes. The cover cost 1/6d (7½p), the addition

587

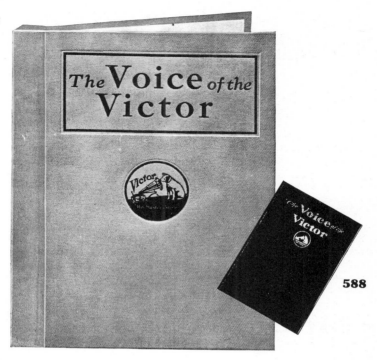

588

589

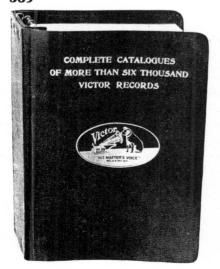

590

591

592

594

593

595

596

597

598

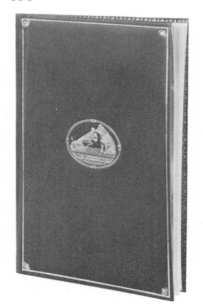

599

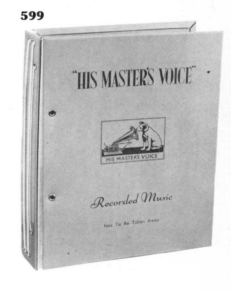

of the Dealer's name and address cost a further 2/6d (12½p) a dozen covers (illus no. 597).

After the War The Gramophone Company produced a newly designed binder to hold the main catalogue and the monthly supplements (illus no. 599). This was covered with plastic and printed in red with gold lettering.

1953 saw a special numerical catalogue holder for the three E.M.I. marks (illus no. 593). The cover was in crocodile finished plastic with gold lettering. The Dealer price was 12/6d (67½p).

Share Certificates, Record Gift Certificates and Record Token Cards

Book and Record Tokens are now a well known feature of the present giving scene. It is probably less well known that the pioneer schemes in the record industry date back as far as 1912 in the U.S. and to the early 1930's in Britain.

The first gift vouchers or 'Gift Certificates' as they were then called, were issued by Wanamaker's, leading New York record Dealers.

Those early certificates were intended to promote and assist the sale of Victor gramophones and records. Wanamaker's explained that the Dealer 'simply filled out and sent the certificate to the person who is to receive the present. The advantage of this method as applied to record presents will be seen at a glance. Not only is the shopper relieved of the necessity of choosing records, but the choice is left with the person who is to receive the records. Consequently the selection is bound to suit the taste of the recipient'.

The certificates had an ornate border but did not bear the Dog Trademark (illus nos 600-601).

Sometime between 1913 and 1918 the Victor Company began to issue its own Certificates. The new design (illus no. 602) now carried the Dog Trademark. The Certificates were issued to Dealers free of charge and included the Dealer's name on each form. This style continued in use until the end of 1920.

In 1921 a third design appeared (illus no. 603) which was to be used for the next two years. Now the border was much more ornate and the Trademark and a Victor Record were prominently featured.

During October 1923 Victor advertised 'The new Christmas Gift Certificate' which they stated 'looks like real money' (illus no. 604). This is by far the most attractive of the series we have found. The border was made up of portraits of famous Victor artists which were printed in colour on excellent quality white paper. The printing had the appearance of a fine steel engraving. The Dog Trademark appears prominently in the centre of the top border. It seems that this fine Certificate continued to be available for at least two more Christmases. The last mention we have of these is for Christmas 1925.

As far as we can tell, the first such items to be issued by The Gramophone Company called 'Christmas Certificates', was during the 1930's (illus no. 605). They measured 8½ inches long × 4½ inches wide and were printed in green and red on cream coloured paper. The Dog Trademark was prominently printed in red on the right hand side of the certificate and repeated in a much smaller size in green on the left hand side. Unlike the Victor certificates they bore a seasonal design being decorated with a border of holly.

The Gramophone Company explained the working of the scheme to its Dealers:

"Christmas Certificates are vouchers provided free to 'His Master's Voice' Dealers for sale to customers who wish to make presents of records to their friends. All the customer has to do is to tell you how much he wishes to

600

601

602

603

VICTOR RECORD CERTIFICATE

Will deliver to _____

VICTOR RECORDS *of any desired selection to the value of* $ _____

_____ 100 **DOLLARS**

May the pleasure derived from these
Victor Records of your own selection
prove as great as the pleasure it affords

_____ *By* _____

in wishing you a very Merry Christmas
and a bright and Happy New Year

604

VICTOR RECORD CERTIFICATE

Will deliver to _____

VICTOR RECORDS *of any desired selection to the value of* $ _____

(_____ 100 *Dollars*)

May the pleasure derived from these Victor Records of your own selection prove as
great as the pleasure it affords _____ *in wishing you*
a very Merry Christmas and a Bright and Happy New Year

_____
DEALER'S SIGNATURE

605

606

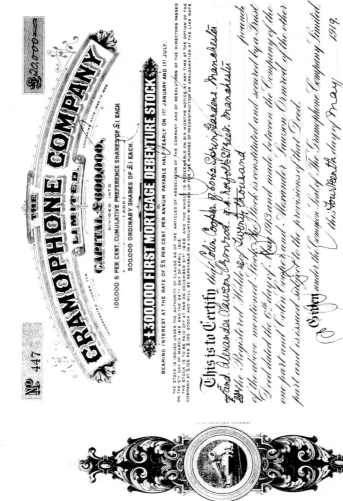

No. 447

£10.000

COMMENCED OCTR 1898 TO 1898

THE
GRAMOPHONE COMPANY
LIMITED

INCORPORATED UNDER

CAPITAL £600,000

DIVIDED INTO

100,000 5 PER CENT. CUMULATIVE PREFERENCE SHARES OF £1 EACH
AND
500,000 ORDINARY SHARES OF £1 EACH.

£300,000 FIRST MORTGAGE DEBENTURE STOCK

BEARING INTEREST AT THE RATE OF 5 PER CENT. PER ANNUM PAYABLE HALF YEARLY ON 1ST JANUARY AND 1ST JULY.

THE STOCK IS ISSUED UNDER THE AUTHORITY OF CLAUSE 49 OF THE ARTICLES OF ASSOCIATION OF THE COMPANY AND OF RESOLUTIONS OF THE DIRECTORS PASSED ON THE 13TH DAY OF MARCH 1915 AND THE 24TH DAY OF APRIL 1915. THE STOCK IS TO BE PAID OFF AT PAR ON DECEMBER 31ST 1938, AND THE WHOLE IS REDEEMABLE ON SIX MONTHS NOTICE AT ANY TIME AT THE OPTION OF THE COMPANY AT £105 PER £100 STOCK AND WILL BE REPAYABLE IN A VOLUNTARY WINDING UP FOR THE PURPOSE OF RECONSTRUCTION OR AMALGAMATION AT THE LIKE RATE.

This is to Certify that Colin Cooper, 5, Zora Spring Gardens, Manchester and Alexander Lawson Conrad, J. A. Royds Street, Manchester

is the Registered Holder of Twenty thousand pounds of the above mentioned Stock. The Stock is constituted and secured by a Trust Deed dated the 6th day of May 1919 and made between the Company of the one part and Colin Cooper and Alexander Lawson Conrad of the other first and issued subject to the provisions of that Deed.

Given under the Common Seal of The Gramophone Company Limited.
this fourteenth day of May 1919.

DIRECTORS.

SECRETARY.

607

spend on each friend, to give you the names and addresses of those friends
and to sign the attractive greeting card which we provide for the purpose.
He — or she — then sends to each friend the appropriate voucher, the
greeting card and the Gift Suggestion booklet from which the selection is
made by the recipient — and when the latter has filled in the Christmas
Certificate with his choice of records and returned it to you — you send the
records.

You should be careful to add to the charge made for the certificate the cost
of packing and carriage, if this should be outside your own delivery area".

These 'Christmas Certificates' were the forerunners of the E.M.I. Record
Token Scheme which was introduced during 1939. It was suspended during the
War and recommenced in 1948.

Series of newly designed Record Token Gift Cards were produced each year.
Strangely, only one reflecting 'Nipper' has been traced; this features the H.M.V.
Dog as 'Dog Toby' with Punch (illus no. 606). This design also appeared on
leaflets and as a poster, with the wording 'Childrens Records'.

All Share Certificates, of any design, are now very collectable. The Gramophone Company, of course, issued numerous Certificates over the years to
coincide with changes of corporate title or increase in Capital etc. As far as we
are aware, none of these Certificates, the earliest of which goes back to 1899,
carry the Dog Trademark. However, a Mortgage Debenture Certificate, dating
from May 1919, shows a change in style and had the Dog Trademark
incorporated in the design at the lefthand margin (illus no. 607).

Postcards

As with so many other aspects of 'Nipperie' making a collection of 'Nipper' orientated postcards brings the gramophone enthusiast into direct competition with the serious general postcard collector, thus making material already in short supply even harder to locate.

'Nipper' related postcards fall into two main categories — firstly 'Trade Cards' sent by the Victor or Gramophone companies to their Dealers and 'Dealer Cards' sent by the Dealer to his customers. Secondly, cards issued by Postcard manufacturers for sale to the public, usually consisting of parodies or variations on the 'His Master's Voice' theme.

The cards of the second group are more often found and most collectors will be familiar with the variants of the 'His Master's VICE' theme. The cards shown in illustrations numbers 608-611 all come from this group.

Trade Postcards are less seldom found and are consequently all the more collectable.

Cards carrying reproductions of the Dog painting are very desirable. The earliest of these Postcard reproductions dates from 1900. By February 1st of that year, The German Company had produced a rough proof of a sample Postcard. The finished card was expected to cost 6 Pfennigs each. This was rejected by the British Company as 'being far too expensive'. However, the move had been made and from then onwards a whole series of 'His Master's Voice' Postcards were issued by the various Branch Companies. Some were reproductions in full colour, others merely in monochrome. Illustration number 613 dates from 1901, number 612 circa 1902, numbers 615-616 circa 1909 and number 614 from the 1950's.

During October 1904 attempts were made by The Gramophone & Typewriter Ltd's factory at Hanover to produce A Gramophone Record Postcard. These experiments apparently consisted of coating an ordinary large size postcard with shellac or with a very thin sheet of transparent celluloid. In the latter case an ordinary pictorial postcard was taken and the celluloid pasted over the picture 'so that the appearance of the card was in no way interfered with'.

It was contemplated that these Special Postcard Records should be released for sale to the public over the 1904 Christmas period. At the same time serious consideration was given to the production of cardboard records and by the beginning of November 1904 some success was achieved in making these. It is not clear if any of the Record Postcards or Cardboard Records actually reached the British market. However some 3,000 Record Postcards were placed on sale in Paris during December 1904.

It is known that in January 1905 Will Gaisberg recorded two special 3 inch diameter recordings whilst in Amsterdam for use on Gramophone Record Postcards and these were probably issued later that year. What illustrations or print appeared on these Record Cards is not known.

608

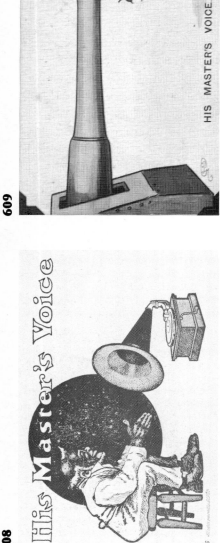

His Master's Voice

609

HIS MASTER'S VOICE.

610

"YOU CAN'T KID ME THAT'S MASTER'S VOICE — WHY I'VE NOT HEARD A SINGLE CUSS-WORD SINCE IT STARTED."

611

WHISKY.

His Master's Breath

614

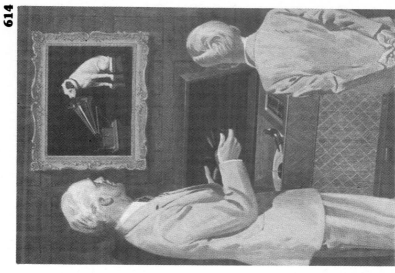

"Since I was your age—A Symbol of Quality"

612

CIE FRANCAISE DU GRAMOPHONE
15, RUE BLEUE, 15

LA VOIX DE SON MAITRE.

613

The Gramophone & Typewriter Lᵗᵈ, 127, Keizersgracht, AMSTERDAM

Er zijn verschillende Spreekmachines; doch er is slechts een Gramophone, die alle andere eclipseert!!

"De stem des Meesters" (Wettig gedeponeerd)

615

616

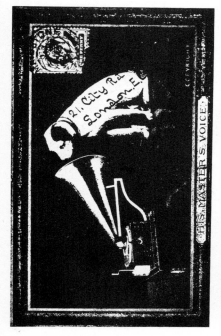

617

618

619

620

621

Reverse side of card

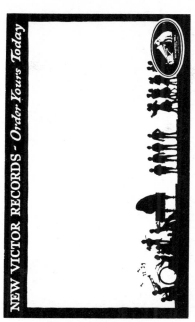

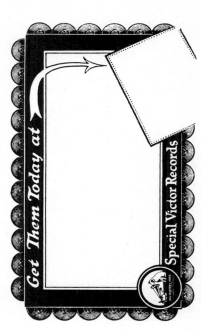

627

628

629

630

"LISTEN TO THE TONE"

"LISTEN TO THE TONE"

"His Master's Voice"
SUPERHET RADIOGRAM SEVEN

"LISTEN TO THE TONE"

"His Master's Voice"
SUPERHET RADIOGRAM FIVE

"His Master's Voice"
SUPERHET CONCERT SEVEN
WITH AUTOMATIC VOLUME CONTROL

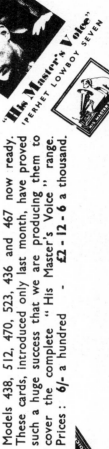

"LISTEN TO

"His Master's Voice"
'PERHET LOWBOY SEVEN

"His Master's Voice"
SUPERHET SELECTIVE F...

Models 438, 512, 470, 523, 436 and 467 now ready. These cards, introduced only last month, have proved such a huge success that we are producing them to cover the complete "His Master's Voice" range.

Prices : **6/-** a hundred - **£2 - 12 - 6** a thousand.

When The Gramophone Company sent special Postcards to all its Dealers via the Coronation First U.K. Aerial Post in 1911 they produced a real find for collectors (illus no. 617).

The cards shown in illustrations numbers 618-621 are all taken from designs used on the front covers of monthly record Supplements. Illustration number 618 dates from 1905 whilst the cards in illustration numbers 619-621 were issued by the Spanish Company in 1909. These reproduce two of the paintings already mentioned in the chapter on 'Christmas Cards, Calendars and Seasonal Pictures'. Similar cards were issued by the British Company in 1908/09. All of these cards gave details of some of the new records to be issued during the month and were obviously intended for Dealers to mail to their customers.

In September 1922 the Victor Company issued sets of six 'Rub In' Victor Postcards. A set of these cards is shown in illustration number 622. In a letter to its Dealers the Victor Company describes how the cards are to be used:

'"Rub 'em, Tub 'em, Scrub 'em, they come out smiling" says a well known manufacturer of womens apparel "Rub 'em they come out with a message" might be said of the rub-in Victor postcards.

The picture to be rubbed in with a coin is part of the story of course . . . Rub the card entitled 'Why are the children so happy?' and the word 'Victrola' with a picture of one of the new models appears. Rub 'What is he carrying in the case?' and a portable Victrola gradually fills in and so on. Each card has a 'tear off' return mailing section. This can be obtained with or without imprint.

As a novelty with a direct selling value the 'rub in' card rates high, because it practically compells the recipient to take a definite action as a result of his curiosity and how many human beings lack that quality? The result of that action is the message. The things a game in a way and all the world loves a game'.

These cards were printed and supplied by the Richardson Illustration Company of New York City at a price of $12.15 for 100 sets (600 cards).

The following year the Victor Company made available to their Dealers a series of electroes for printing postcards with their own sales messages. The eight cards in illustration numbers 623-630 show some of the designs before the Dealer material had been added.

Cards showing aerial views of The Gramophone Company's Hayes Factory complex, How to get to Hayes, New Radio and TV Models and Artist Portrait cards etc. must have been issued in their thousands. Cards shown in illustration number 631 are examples of this genre. They were printed in two colours and date from 1934.

Some of these cards would have had an ordinary postcard reverse with listings of records or sales blurb printed on the message area. Others would have had the text printed right across the reverse side.

Regrettably no one seems to have kept a record of the postcard designs prepared and printed for the Victor and Gramophone Companies. This means that every find may be a new discovery and this all adds to the fascination of the subject.

Stationery/Promotional Stamps and Seals

We feel that some mention should be made of stationary on which the H.M.V. Dog appears. Most pieces coming into collectors hands will probably have originated from local H.M.V. Record and Radio Dealers, letters, bill headings etc. Any of these are now worth preserving, especially those carrying the H.M.V. Trademark.

Even more interesting are letters and envelopes coming from the various record companies themselves. A collection of Gramophone or Victor Company letter headings through the years would be a prized acquisition. The Gramophone Company, of course, had Branch Houses around the world and letter headings from any or all of these, in their various languages and local styles would also be very desirable.

Dealer's aids or customer gifts, pens, pencils, etc. are also very collectable but, alas, now seldom found.

In this chapter we can merely suggest certain lines for investigation and collection when the opportunity exists.

Coloured seals or stamps for affixing onto envelopes, letters or bills have been in use by the record companies for many years. Anyone coming upon examples of these items should most certainly preserve them.

Illustration number 633 dates from 1913. It was printed in red and makes a bright and attractive splash of colour.

The German Branch of The Gramophone Company issued the stamp in illustration number 638 in 1912 and that in illustration number 637 in 1914.

We have no exact dates for illustration numbers 634-635. The former is attractive and printed in full colours. Both probably date from the end of the early 1920's.

In 1934 The Gramophone Company started 'The Record of the Month' campaign. The stamps in illustration numbers 639-640 were part of this effort.

The seal in illustration number 636 was printed in red and black and comes from 1938/39.

The only modern example (illus no. 632) is from the 1960's.

Dealers would often be supplied with special letter headings, sales letters,envelopes etc., by both the Victor and Gramophone Companies.

Illustration number 641 dates from 1920 and number 644 from 1921. The Gramophone Company's Dealers heading for 1938 is shown in illustration number 643.

The H.M.V. adhesive tape and rubber stamp date from 1934/38 (illus nos. 648-649). The rubber stamp cost Dealers 2/- (10p) each.

Special H.M.V. pencils could be obtained from The Gramophone Company carrying the H.M.V. Trademark and the Dealer's name and address. These were available through 1934/38 at 12/6d (62½p) a gross (illus no. 647).

The ball pen and pencil in illustration numbers 650-651 date from the 1960's.

632

633

634

635

637

636

638

639

640

641

642

643

NATIONAL MUSIC ROLL CO.

Name

Amount

LITTLE FALLS FELT SHOE CO.

Name

Amount

Join Our Victrola Club

14 Cents A Day

Is all it costs you to buy a genuine Victrola. We deliver the Victrola when you make the first payment.

All models from $25. to $150. Any finish to match your furniture.

Don't accept a substitute, look inside the lid. If it hasn't this trade-mark, it isn't a Victrola. We are exclusive Victor Agents.

Henry Taubman,   St. Johnsville, N. Y.

644

645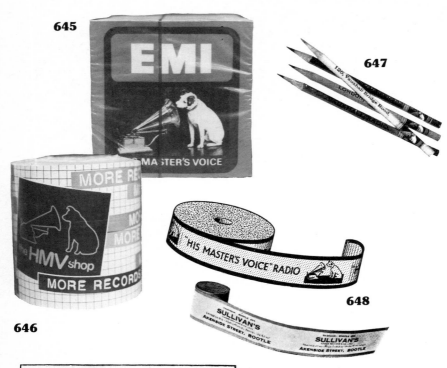

647

646

648

649

650

651

The pen cost 2/9d (14p) and the pencil 3/2d (16p).

More recently The Gramophone Company made available an attractive EMI/HMV message block (illus no. 645) and during the period 1980/83 HMV Record Shops produced a 'More Rock than . . .' message block, with a hole at the top to hold a pencil (ilus no. 646). The design was similar to the 'More Rock than . . .' mug illustrated in the chapter on 'Useful and Acceptable Gifts'.

Cartoons

The earliest known 'Nipper' cartoon appeared in the American publication 'Judge' in 1902 when Theodore Roosevelt was President of the U.S.A. It was drawn by Victor Gillam (illus no. 652). Since that time month by month, year by year, new cartoons on the 'His Master's Voice' 'Nipper' theme have appeared around the world.

Compiling a collection of 'Nipper' cartoons can be an interesting and rewarding project and, what is more, it costs almost nothing to indulge. All you have to do is to clip out any 'Nipper' orientated cartoon you happen to see in newspapers and magazines. If you're lucky enough to have any friends, get them to search out cartoons in the newspapers and magazines that *they* take. Overseas acquaintances can be particularly valuable in this respect.

A 'Nipper' Scrapbook compiled by one of the authors over many years has made numerous television appearances and seems to be still in demand.

Never neglect to look through old newspapers and magazines, you never know when and where you will discover new 'Nipper' material. Newspaper cartoonists are particularly fond of 'Nipper' and you will soon find which magazines are most likely to yield up material. 'Punch' of course, is a rich source.

Of course, if you want to be really grand you can always set out to collect the artist's original drawing or artwork. Sir Joseph Lockwood, Chairman of EMI for twenty years, tells us that he has a large collection of these original drawings, mostly presented to him by the artists. We lesser mortals can not, of course, expect such largesse, although it is still possible to obtain such prizes. If you see a cartoon that pleases you, do not hesitate, make contact with the artist, (you can do this through his paper or magazine Publishing House) asking if the original drawing is still available and if it is for sale.

Some of the drawings will have been done on scraps of paper, others on A4 sheets and still others as formal artwork mounted on card.

It is difficult to say what you might expect to pay; it will greatly depend upon the subject, size and the name of the artist. You should probably allow at least £60 although some small items may be cheaper, certainly the large major cartoons will cost more.

We regret that copyright problems have precluded the inclusion of illustrations of modern 'Nipper' cartoons.

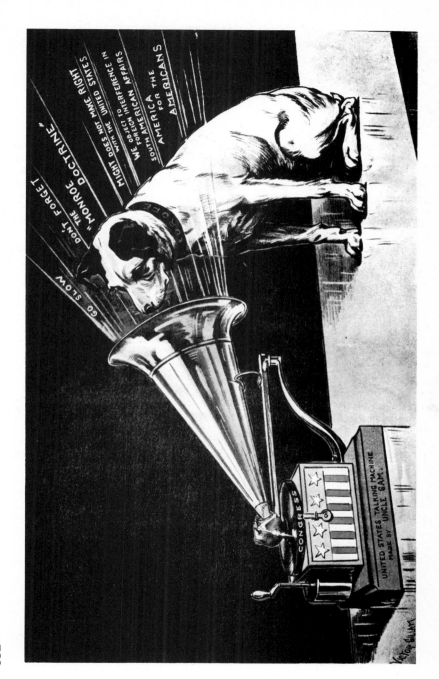

652

Nipper in Verse and Prose

Although the authors have, in the past, seen various examples of 'Nipper' in verse, regrettably no special note was made of them and they have now mostly vanished from our knowledge. However, these six, five in verse, the other in prose, have been retraced and are reproduced below. Those of you who are of a sentimental disposition be warned, the words you will read are somewhat maudlin and melodramatic. They may well bring a lump to your throat and tears to your eyes. So, dear reader, 'if you have tears to shed, prepare to shed them now'.

In 1900 a poem, well a sort of poem, entitled 'His Master's Voice (Suggested by the picture)' came into being. The author very wisely hid his, or her, identity behind the letters J.G. From its date we would think that this must be one of the earliest poems on the subject.

HIS MASTER'S VOICE *(Suggested by the picture)*

Which this history is pathetic so prepare to shed your tears
for it treats of dead mens' voices heard across the gulf of years.
It will harrow up your feelings — it will set your nerves arack,
Will this story of a man whose voice long after death came back.
Jones was hale and well at thirty, and his clothes (anglice 'togs')
Indicated that this life was lived for horses — likewise dogs.
But of all his dogs and horses — there was one that he'd picked up
On the course one day at Sandown — just a half bred Yorkshire Pup.
Jones became devoted to it — doggie whined were he away,
Whined a cadence, sombre dirgey, whined in fact through night and day,
And when neighbours told him of it, he was really very pleased
And expressed himself delighted — but they somehow weren't appeased.
Another trait possessed he, Jones to music was inclined,
And he often longed to hear some, more especially when he dined.
He was fair upon the cornet — and the flute he sometimes tried,
But those who heard his trombone either took to drink or died.
He was humming in a shop one day a song about a coon
When an evil genius whispered in his ear the word 'bassoon'
"By jove the very thing I want" he said "for solid tone"
"Excuse me" said the shopman "what you want's a Gramophone".
"A Gramophone!" exclaimed he "why what is that perchance?"
"It's a solo" said the salesman, "it's an organ, it's a dance,
It's an orchestra, a lullaby, a coon song for your honey
And it's Five Pound Ten with fixings" and Jones planked down his money.
Jones took a violent fancy to this trumpet on a cube,
He made speeches after dinner which he spokes into the tube,

And as he heard his periods rolling out in accents grand
He smiled with pride superior — the mongrel also took a hand.
These days of halcyon bliss sped by, then Jones one day got ill
A fever caught him tightly and held him with a will.
They tried him hard with nitre — in blankets he was wrapped
But efforts all were useless — the chain of life was snapped.
The dog (here starts the pathos) sat beside his grave for years,
It ate not and it drank not, except its own salt tears.
It was getting thinner looking, its face with lines was serried
But it wouldn't leave the spot wherein its still loved boss lay buried.
One day an inspiration struck the heir of William Jones
"The Gramophone" he muttered, "I will try its tender tones
The Gramophone — I'll try it, if that fails I'll give it up".
Then he laid the wondrous instrument beside the sickly pup.
He wound it up — a voice spake out, "Come hither gentle dog
Come hither to your master, while he serves you out your prog".
The dog looked up all wondering, and his eyes shon clear and bright
'Twas his master's voice had spoken and he yelped in fierce delight.
Yelped and skipped about in gladness — he was happy — he had heard
His Master's Voice by proxy, then he died without a word.
Which only shows dear readers — and this verse shall be my last,
That whatever may be told you, th'age of miracles is not past.

J.G.

We suppose the apocryphal story of Francis Barraud's original painting showing 'Nipper' sitting on his master's coffin must have had a profound effect upon its hearers who immediately rushed into print with pathetic verse or prose.

If you are not too flushed and tearful to continue reading further, we would commend your attention to an advertisement which appeared in 'Hondenrassen' (Dog Breeds) which was published in Brussels during September 1904. The advertisement seems to have been inserted by the Belgian Branch of The Gramophone and Typewriter Ltd and the copy written by H.A. Graaf Van Bylandt.

HIS MASTER'S VOICE

He was a bit funny, but otherwise a very likeable chap, was our friend 'Kees' (i.e. Cornelius). All alone in the world, he was a bachelor ever since he had had a narrow escape from the meshes of feminine guile, a bachelor that sought compensation for the lack of a home of his own in the circle of some other jolly fellows.

'Kees' was the life and soul of the little club, being as inexhaustible in inventing jokes as he was inimitable in cracking them.

One of the members of the club was Mr X of the Gramophone & Typewriter Ltd., through whom 'Kees' spoke some of the jokes into the gramophone.

Apart from his friends, 'Kees' also had a dog, which goes without saying, a rarely intelligent animal called 'Fox', which was the favourite of all of us, and the idol of 'Kees'. 'Fox' understood every word his master said, and when the latter cracked a joke, the dog would follow him closely and as the joke neared its point, 'Fox' would start stroking his own snout with his paw and begin to sneeze and at the right moment, without fail, he would, by barking fiercely, give the signal for a general outburst of laughter, and in so doing would sometimes jump several feet up in the air. Then, after the storm of laughter had subsided and silence had returned once more, 'Fox' could all of a sudden be heard to growl softly, shaking his head as though he wanted to say 'Boss, boss, you are absolutely priceless, you are unique, do please, stop now'.

One day we were sitting at our club-table and were vainly waiting for our friend, but 'Kees' did not turn up, for he was ill. Within a few days his condition was hopeless and after a week 'Kees' was dead. There was general depression and after we had seen our dear friend to his last resting place, we first of all gathered round the club-table again, where we found 'Fox' already sitting on his master's chair, a picture of deep sorrow. Tears came into our eyes at the sight of that poor animal; the dog was a mere shadow of the 'Fox' of former days, and no matter how hard we tried to cheer him up, it was all in vain. 'Fox' had not tasted any food since his master's death and it was to be foreseen that he would not survive the latter for long.

Suddenly Mr X of the Gramophone & Typewriter Ltd., hits on the idea of calling on the gramophone for help; among general approval, this latter is set up and one of the records made by 'Kees' is played. No sooner are the first few words to be heard in the room than 'Fox' suddenly wakes from his depression pricks up his ears and stares like mad at the gramophone. Life, already departing, is returning to him. Now comes the point (i.e. of a joke on the record). Everybody is holding his breath. All of a sudden, loud laughter pours forth from the horn. 'Fox' has got up on his legs and is joining in the uproar, barking his head off. The friends forget the part they are supposed to play and join in. 'Fox' is lifted on to the table and set before the gramophone and another record by his boss is played back. 'Fox' comes to life even more, wagging his tail; he lets himself be stroked by us and in his elation even takes a bit of sausage which has been offered to him, and while 'Fox' is eating, Mr X puts on another record by 'Kees' and — the attempt met with complete success. 'Fox' recovered and became his old self again after having been saved by the gramophone, and every evening he came along to listen to HIS MASTER'S VOICE. Such is, briefly, the story of the birth of our well known record: 'HIS MASTER'S VOICE'.
The Gramophone & Typewriter Ltd
Head office for Holland; Amsterdam, 566 Heerengracht Tel 3545
Cable address: 'Soundbox'

The Germans seem to have taken considerable interest in the 'His Master's Voice' theme. During 1900 both Hermann Bottcher (41139) and Martin Bendix (41142X) made 7 inch recordings of pieces entitled 'Die Stimme seines Herrn'.

In 1905 the Band of the 43rd Infantry Regiment of Koenigsberg recorded Charmes de Sirène (Waldteufel) which included the barking of a human (?)dog. This was quite shamelessly reissued in Britain on GC 2-100 as 'His Master's Voice' March (with barking by the Gramophone Dog) and played by the Royal Military Band. The entry in the February 1905 Supplement is shown in illustration number 653.

During 1952 RCA Victor issued a 45 rpm disc of 'Little Nipper Riddles' and 'The Little Nipper March'.

10-INCH
CONCERT RECORDS.

5/= each.

BAND SELECTIONS.

Band of H.M. Coldstream Guards.
Conductor, Lieut. J. Mackenzie Rogan (Hon. R.A.M.).
G.C. 2—67   The Jolly Coppersmiths Polka (*Peter*).
G.C. 2—101 Hoch Habsburg March (*Kral*).
G.C. 2—102 Masonic March, introducing   "Onward,
               Christian Soldiers."

The Royal Military Band.
G.C. 2—100 "His Master's Voice" March.
    (With barking by the Gramophone dog.)

Bohemian Orchestra.
G.C. 724 Dixie land (two-step) (*Haines*).

Niederschlesischen Infantry Regiment Band.
   These are exceptionally fine records.
G.C. 2—40115 Forget-me-not (*Macbeth*).
G.C. 2—40116 Italy Marcia (*Minoliti*).
G.C. 2—40117 Des Kaiser's Liebgarde (*Nitzsche*).
G.C. 2—40119 Tritt gefasst Marsch (*Windisch*).

Pryor's Band.
V.M. 2—103 Japanese National Air (now being played at
            Tokio).
V.M. 2—104 Any Rags Schottische.

Spanish Gipsy Orchestra.
G.C. 60248. Sardana—La Pubilla Ampordanesa (*Serra*).
G.C. 60254   ,,   Ayre, Ayre.

CONCERT MUSIC.

Mr. Stanley Kirkby (Baritone).
G.C. 3—2176 Cigarette, "Catch of the Season" (*Haines*).

Mr. J. B. Macklane (Scotch Tenor).
G.C. 3—2177 Be kind to auld Grannie.

Mr. John McCormack (Irish Tenor).
G.C. 3—2168 Snowy-breasted Pearl (*Robinson*).
G.C. 3—2169 Killarney (violin obligato) (*Balfe*).
G.C. 3—2170 Come back to Erin (violin obligato).
G.C. 3—2171 The Foggy Dew (*V. Stanford*).

Mr. Griffiths Percy (Bass).
   Accompanied by Band of H.M. Coldstream Guards.
G.C. 3—2178 God Save The King.

Madame Alice Esty (Operatic Soprano).
          12-inch Records.
03038 Breeze of the Night (*Trovatore*).
03039 Elsa's Dream, "Lohengrin" (*Wagner*).

Miss Elizabeth Parkina (Soprano).
G.C. 3581 When you speak to me (*Guy d'Hardelot*).
G.C. 3584 'Tis the day (*Leoncavallo*).

COMIC SONG .

Mr. Harry Lauder.
G.C. 3—2174 The Wedding of Lauchie McGraw.
G.C. 3—2175 A Trip to Inverary.
           — —
   (With full Military Band accompaniment.)
G.C. 3—2179 Early in the morning.
G.C. 3—2180 Stop your tickling, Jock.

SERIO-COMIC SONGS.

Miss Florrie Forde.
G.C. 3578 Jack, Jack, Jack.
G.C. 3579 Crackling of the Pork.

Miss Queenie Leighton.
   (As sung by her at Drury Lane Pantomime.)
G.C. 3577 Love's Gramophone.

DUETS.

Messrs. Stanley Kirkby and Ernest Pike.
G.C. 4356 Tenor and Baritone (*Wilson*).
G.C. 4357 Love and War (*Cooke*).
G.C. 4358 Excelsior (*Balfe*).

INSTRUMENTALISTS.

VIOLIN.

Miss Marie Hall.
G.C. 7986 Humoreske (*Anton Dvorák*).
G.C. 7989 Perpetuum Mobile, Op. 34 (*Ries*).
G.C. 7990 Excerpt from Finale Mendelssohn's Concerto.

BANJO DUET.

Messrs. Ossman and Hunter.
V.M. 6453 Navajo (Indian two-step).

PICCOLO.

Mr. Frank Mazziotta.
V.M. 9032 Patrol Comique.

SAXOPHONE.

M. Jeans Moeremans.
V.M. 9365 Carnival of Venice.

WHISTLING.

M. Guido Gialdini.
G.C. 49287 Habanera, "Carmen."

*These records should be played with genuine Gramophone needles, which are sold only in metal boxes bearing our copyright picture, "His Master's Voice," on the lid.
No genuine Gramophone needles are sold in paper packets.*

Der verwunderte Fox.

"Nanu, du bist wohl nicht gesund?"
Spricht zum Gramola hier der Hund.
"Wo hast du deinen Trichter nur?"
Ich seh' von ihm nicht eine Spur. — —"

— "Den Trichter hab' ich innerlich — —"

— "Nee", sagt der Hund, "das glaub ich nich.
Du wirst wohl auch nicht singen können.
Und wie soll ich dich denn benennen.
Ein Grammophon bist du doch nicht."

Da lacht's Gramola laut und spricht:
"Mein lieber Freund, halb hast du recht,
Doch meine Kunst ist wahr und echt.

Gramola werde ich genannt,
Bin schon bekannt im ganzen Land."
Und damit fing es an zu klingen —
Da muss' der Hund vor Freuden springen —

"Ei, ei, wie schön ist dieser Ton,
Fast schöner als beim Grammophon
Doch eines muss ich dich noch fragen,
Kannst du auch meinen Namen sagen?"

Und "Fox" ertönt es laut und tief,
Genau, als ob der Hund ihn rief.

Da sprach der Hund: "Das hör' ich gern,
Das war die Stimme meines Herrn."
A. F.

Die Stimme seines Herrn.

Ein düstres Zimmer, in der Ecke
Ein aufgewühltes leeres Bett,
Daneben Fox auf woll'ner Decke,
Fast abgemagert zum Skelet. —
So liegt er da schon seit zwei Tagen
Und blickt ganz traurig um sich her,
Weil seinen Herrn man fortgetragen,
Drum nimmt er auch kein Futter mehr.

Die Köchin weiss sich nicht zu raten,
Die Träne rollt ihr ins Gesicht;
Sie streichelt ihn, sie gibt ihm Braten,
Jedoch der Fox, er rührt sich nicht.
Da plötzlich kommt ihr ein Gedanke,
Vom seel'gen Herrn das Grammophon
Holt freudig, schnell sie aus dem Schranke,
Und bald ertönt mit lautem Ton
Ein Pfiff; der Hund reckt seine Glieder,
Die Ohren spitzt das treue Tier,
Da tönt es aus dem Trichter wieder:
"Komm her, mein Fox, komm her zu mir!"

Da fühlt er in sich neues Leben,
Zum Tische ist er hingerannt,
Es hat der treue Fox soeben —
Die Stimme seines Herrn erkannt.
Vor Freude kann das Tier kaum schnaufen,
Die Köchin glaubt ihn schon gesund,
Doch als das Uhrwerk abgelaufen,
Da sinkt zusammen auch der Hund. —
Sie sieht die treuen Augen brechen,
Als möchten sie zum Abschied gern
Noch wie ein Mensch die Worte sprechen:
"Ich folg' der Stimme meines Herrn!"

Henry Bender

Wohl wenig Schutzmarken sind in Deutschland so schnell und wirkungsvoll bekannt geworden wie unser Hund vor dem Grammophon. — Es sind jetzt gerade 10 Jahre, dass dieses treffende Symbol der Deutschen Grammophon A.-G. als Schutzbezeichnung ihrer Erzeugnisse dient, und diejenigen unserer Leser, welche bereits seit dieser Zeit im Besitze eines Grammophons sind, werden sich sicherlich noch des eigenartigen Gedichts erinnern, das damals auf dieses Symbol die genannte Gesellschaft veröffentlichte, und das trotz des "ernsten Inhalts" aus der Feder unsres allbekannten und allbeliebten Humoristen Henry Bender stammt.

Nummer 1   Januar 1914   VII. Jahrgang **656**

Offizielle „Grammophon" Nachrichten

Herausgegeben durch die DEUTSCHE GRAMMOPHON-AKTIENGESELLSCHAFT zu Berlin S.42, Ritterstr.35

Diese Zeitschrift erscheint am 1. eines jeden Monats. Der Nachdruck sämtlicher Artikel — Interessenten erhalten ein Exemplar kostenlos zugesandt — mit Quellenangabe ist gestattet.

657

Unseren Händlern zum neuen Jahre!

DIE STIMME SEINES HERRN

Im Jahrgang Num'ro Sieben
Ist Fox getreu zur Stell',
Begrüßt all' seine Lieben
Mit freundlichem Gebell.
„Das alte Jahr war böse,"
So mancher Händler schwur,
Da gab es Kriegsgetöse
Und schlechte Konjunktur."
Doch Fox ist andrer Meinung,
Grad' dann hört jeder gern
— Trotz schüchterner Verneinung —
Die Stimme seines Herrn.
Wenn wüst im Weltgetümmel
Ein Hader artet aus,
Dann schafft man sich den Himmel
In seinem eignen Haus. —

Seid nur zu jeder Stunde
Der Neuheit Interpret,
Dann klopft schon an der Kunde
Und wünscht die Novität.
Er klopft auch immer wieder,
Der Reiz bleibt dauerhaft,
Es üben Spiel' und Lieder
Magnetisch starke Kraft.
Ich geb' Euch voll Vertrauen
Auch dies Jahr das Geleit,
Um felsenfest zu bauen
Auf Eure Reglamkeit.
Nichts wird den Lohn verkürzen,
Der Händler wird besteh'n.
Heil 1914!
Ich gratuliere schön!

This was issued to tie in with a tremendous year long campaign and a sixty day Little Nipper Contest to promote childrens records in the U.S.A. The attractive record cover announced the contest, gave the simple rules and provided space for the contestant to answer the riddles as well as to tell why he or she wanted a Little Nipper Puppy. The prizes for the winners were 100 live puppy dogs, and 1,000 rubber replicas of Nipper.

In 1910 Henry Bender, a famous German comic and recording artist, wrote his version of 'Die Stimme seines Herrn' (illus no. 655).

The February 1912 issue of 'Die Stimme seines Herrn' featured A.T.'s verse (illus no. 654).

The front cover of 'Offizielle Grammophon Nachrichten' for January 1914 again featured Nipper (illus no. 656).

Some twenty-four years later Arthur F. Thorn penned 'A Terrier's Tale':

> There never was a terrier yet
>   Whose fame has spread like mine,
> Whose photograph and statuette
>   Are reported so fine,
> I am the pet of 'HMV',
>   A Record terrier you'll agree!
>
> 'Twas I that first did hear the voice
>   Of Master on the gramophone,
> And was deceived: I had no choice,
>   So natural was the tone.
> I cocked my head and listened well;
>   The difference was hard to tell.
>
> The fact that I was first deceived
>   By scientific voice vibrations,
> Has led, I'm sure you'll be relieved,
>   To universal jubilations.
> From China round to Timbuctoo
>   You'll find my photograph on view.
>
> Each moment in the Empire wide,
>   My well-known figure turns around
> Upon the discs that we provide
>   To carry every wondrous sound;
> And you may hear in forest dark
>   The voice of Melba, as the lark.
>
> In frozen places of the earth,
>   Where sunshine seldom paints the day,
> Where men are wearied by the dearth
>   Of souls that sing and dance and play,
> To gloomy places such as these
>   We send the discs that always please.

It may not be that I shall see
Each face that owes its happy smile
To products made by 'HMV'
That tedium beguile.
But this I know: that all rejoice
When listening to 'His Master's Voice'.
Arthur F. Thorn

Nipper made an attempt to appear on the 'silver screen' when, on August 22nd 1912 Herbert Samuel Berliner, the son of Emile Berliner and Vice President and General Manager of The Berliner Gramophone Company of Canada, applied to Register his Film Play 'The Story of a Famous Picture (L'Histoire d'un Tableau Célèbre)'. Attached to his application was an outline of the plot which was deposited with the Public Records Office in London, where that indefatigable researcher, Frank Andrews, found it and sent one of the writers a xerox copy from which we reprint the following text:

THE STORY OF A FAMOUS PICTURE
(L'Histoire d'un Tableau Celebre)
by
Herbert Samuel Berliner

SCENE: A poorly furnished garret containing a bed, table, on which is sitting a cheap gramophone, and under it a fox terrier after the well known picture, (sleeping) the usual accessories including half a dozen oil paintings along the floor, around the sides of the walls, and also an easel containing a blank canvas, and artist's materials lying around.

The artist, fully dressed, enters, carrying what is ostensibly a picture wrapped up in a newspaper, which he throws down with a gesture of disappointment. The artist also throws down his hat, seats himself at the table, leans with his elbows on same, and presents a picture of utter discouragement. After sitting in this position for a few moments the artist rises and begins to pace the floor. He finally goes over and opens the drawer of the table and pulls out a revolver which he examines when suddenly, his eyes fall upon the gramophone whereupon he lays down the revolver and puts on a record which starts to play. While it is playing he starts to pace up and down the floor again. The dog meanwhile jumps up on to the table and assumes the position as in the trade mark. The artist's eyes fall upon it and he looks vacantly at it and then a look of understanding comes across his face. He claps his hands to his head as if he has an idea and immediately pulls off his coat, picks up his palette, paints and brushes, and then begins to paint. The scene is supposed to continue for the whole night showing early in the morning the finished picture with the artist gazing at it with a critical look.

THE SECOND SCENE: Shows a large business office containing a table around which are seated three or four prosperous looking men. On cabinets around the room are various styles of horn gramophones also a large safe. It is ostensibly a Directors' meeting and the men are discussing things which can be seen by their motions. A page enters bearing a card. One of the men looks at it and motions the page to show the man in.

The artist enters carrying a picture wrapped up in newspaper. The men around the table have in the meanwhile busied themselves discussing matters, and at first pay no attention to the artist who stands waiting with his hat in his hand.

At last the meeting seems to have finished its discussion and one of the men shows the artist in and asks his business. The artist goes through the motions of showing that he has a picture which he desires to show. The other men have risen, and are getting ready to leave. The man talking to the artist at last indicates that he desires to have him unwrap the picture. The man looks at it, seems to be very much surprised and taken with the picture. He calls to the other men excitedly to come to look at it, which they do, and each by his motions shows very plainly that he is very much impressed. This continues for a few moments and then the first man again speaks with the artist, and the conversation ends with a consultation with the other men, after which the first goes over to the safe, opens it and beings out ten packages each of which is marked One Thousand Dollars. These packages are supposed to be notes, not coin. The artist bows his gratitude and thanks, and departs with much alacrity.

THE LAST SCENE: shows the dining room in a cafe with the artist seated with some friends around the table, one patting the dog, drinking Champagne and eating, and making merry. He seems to be describing the picture and they all applaud.

The picture closes with a scene of revelry, followed by throwing on to the screen the picture of 'His Master's Voice' in colours.

Whether the film was actually made we can not say. It would certainly be interesting to see what the director made of it.

Herbert Berliner also suggested that the plot could be used for a stage production.

Years later 'Nipper' did reach the stage, at least by title. On November 10th 1977 the premiere of a new Rock Musical 'His Master's Voice' by David Anderson took place at The Adam Smith Centre at Kirkcaldy (illus no. 658). The production came to London some years later and opened at The Half Moon Theatre, Stepney Green, on October 10th 1983. Illustration number 659 shows the somewhat offensive publicity for the 1983 production, although the idea of the drawing was far from new, a number of similar efforts having appeared over previous years.

The musical was the story of a young punk singer who gets 'discovered' by a record company and offered a contract. The cast included Gary Holton and Gary Shail, who played the main character Wally Burke.

One further item is on our list for inclusion here. Chaliapine singing at midnight in a Moscow tenement. A ballet girl's mysterious visit in the small hours to the house of an elderly admirer. Secret Societies, life behind the scenes in Soviet Russia and red murder at midnight are all ingredients in Ivy Low's novel 'His Master's Voice' published by Heineman at 7/6d in 1930 (illus no. 657). The book has absolutely nothing to do with 'Nipper', however the title intrigued us and it might amuse collectors to pick up any copy of the book they may stumble across.

The Adam Smith Centre KIRKCALDY

Saturday, November 5 at 8 p.m.

HELEN McARTHUR with
BERNARD SUMNER at the piano
Tickets: £1.10, £1.20. No reductions

Tuesday & Wednesday, November 8 and 9, at 7.30 p.m.
THE SCOTTISH BALLET in

BALLET FOR SCOTLAND '77
Tickets: £1.30, £1.50. Students and Senior Citizens ½ price.

Thursday, November 10 until Saturday, November 12—
Thursday and Friday, 7.30; Saturday at 8.00 p.m.
7:84 THEATRE COMPANY presents
"THE PREMIER OF A NEW ROCK MUSICAL"

"HIS MASTER'S VOICE"
by DAVID ANDERSON

Tickets: £1.10, £1.20. Students and Senior Citizens ½ Price Friday 11th.
Two for the price of one Thursday, 10th, 7.30 p.m.

Tuesday, November 15 until Saturday, November 19—
PITLOCHRY FESTIVAL THEATRE
in the brilliant comedy by ALAN AYCKBOURN

RELATIVELY SPEAKING
"An evening of non-stop laughter"

Tuesday to Friday, 7.30 p.m. Saturday, 5.00 p.m. and 8.00 p.m.
Tickets: £1.10, £1.20. Students and Senior Citizens ½ Price Wednesday to Friday. Two for the price of one Tues., 7.30. Sat. at 5.00 p.m.

Book now for the SPECTACULAR FAMILY PANTOMIME

MOTHER GOOSE
Commences December 19 until January 28, 1978

HIS MASTER'S VOICE

A MUSICAL PLAY BY DAVID ANDERSON

From OCTOBER 10
HALF MOON THEATRE
790 4000 ⊖ STEPNEY GREEN

Finding 'Nipper's' Double

In these days of H.M. The Queen and Mrs Thatcher look-alikes and sound-alikes it was almost inevitable that the very superior dog who spends his time listening to His Master's Voice, should want his own look-alike double. Certainly, owning a real live 'Nipper' look-alike may well have considerable appeal to many collectors.

During 1950 The Gramophone Company's Australian Company introduced a new small radio receiver which they honoured with the name of 'Little Nipper'.

To give it a good send off they organized a nationwide competition to find 'Nipper's' double. 'Does your pup look like Nipper' became the catchphrase of the competition and twenty-five of the new receivers were offered as prizes to the competitors whose dogs most resembled Francis Barraud's terrier.

Over 3,500 entries were received. Illustration numbers 661-663 show three of the Australian winners.

The New Zealand Company organized a similar competition which brought in a flood of enquiries. Illustration number 660 shows the New Zealand judges sorting through some of the entries. The winner of the New Zealand competition (illus no. 664) can, we think, truly be regarded as a very near 'Nipper'.

In 1951 Hamilton's Radio House, Hamilton, sent The Gramophone Company a photograph of their 'Nipper' look-alike (illus no. 665).

During 1981 HMV Record Shops Limited in association with The Daily Mirror, organized a National 'Nipper' Contest in Britain. Readers who had a dog looking like the original 'Nipper' were asked to send a picture of him to the organizers at the Daily Mirror Offices. The winner was promised a ride in an open coach with Manchester's Lord Mayor and many other exotic appearances at the various HMV Record Shops around the country.

Hundreds of photographs were examined and eight potential 'Nippers' were finally pulled out of the pile. The winner was a five year old Jack Russell belonging to Mrs Jackie Pritchard of Doncaster — not a 'Nipper' but a 'TOBY' (illus no. 666). Since that time Toby has appeared with some of the greatest pop stars, he even managed to muzzle in with a former Miss World, and that can't be bad!

If your own pet happens to be a Nipper-Look-Alike he may not become as famous as Toby, the new HMV Dog, never the less you will be able to treasure him as your own special Gramophone Dog.

660

661

662

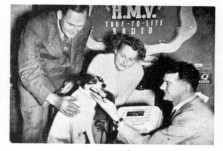

664

663

665

666

Cardboard, Plaster, Papier Mache, Plastic and China Models of Nipper

There can be little doubt that the most popular and successful of all the 'Nipper' souvenirs is the three dimensional model of the Dog. Over the years this has been produced in a whole variety of sizes and models by both the Victor and Gramophone Companies.

As far as we can trace, the earliest representation of 'Nipper' for Dealers showrooms and windows were flat printed cut-outs. In 1907 the Victor Company produced a 19 inch × 19 inch dog. It was intended to be used with a Victor Machine (illus no. 669). Just in case a Dealer was tempted to use the Dog without a Victor machine a Dog and Gramophone cut-out was also produced (illus no. 667). This measured 7½ inches × 15½ inches.

By the end of 1908 the German Branch of The Gramophone Company was presenting its own copy of the Victor cardboard Dog (illus no. 668). Presumably the British Company produced a similar model although we have not seen one of these.

During May 1912 The British Gramophone Company were becoming concerned that not only some of their Dealers, even their own Branch Companies were reversing the Trademark by placing the Dog on the opposite side of the Gramophone to that shown in the original picture. A stern rebuke was dispatched to 'those who had been guilty of this practice', pointing out that this was wrong and that it must stop forthwith.

Probably for similar reasons, in September 1913 the Victor Company made available a new cardboard model Dog which came with its own Gramophone (illus no. 670).

We are not certain when the first three dimensional statue of 'Nipper' was produced for Dealer distribution. The earliest reference we have traced is in the Spring of 1913 when the Berlin Sales Office of the Gramophone Company's German Branch submitted to London a sample papier mache Dog with an estimate for supplying them at 8/- (40p) each in quantities of 100. The British Company 'Decided not to entertain the idea' and it is not known whether the German Company actually went into production with these models.

Two years later whilst Britain was busily engaged in fighting the Great War against Germany, the Overseas Department of the Company memoed that it was having some model plaster Dogs made at a cost of 2/6d (12½p) each. The size of these is unknown. The British Sales Committee agreed to inspect a sample of this new model 'owing to the very poor models of our Trademark previously submitted'. Once again it is unknown whether these were made for the British market, or even produced at all.

In 1916 The Victor Company produced a large model of the 'Victor' Dog which was placed on top of the 'Dome of Music' at the Panama-Pacific Exposition. This created so much interest among Dealers and public that arrangements were made with the Old King Cole Papier Mache Works, Canton,

667

668

669

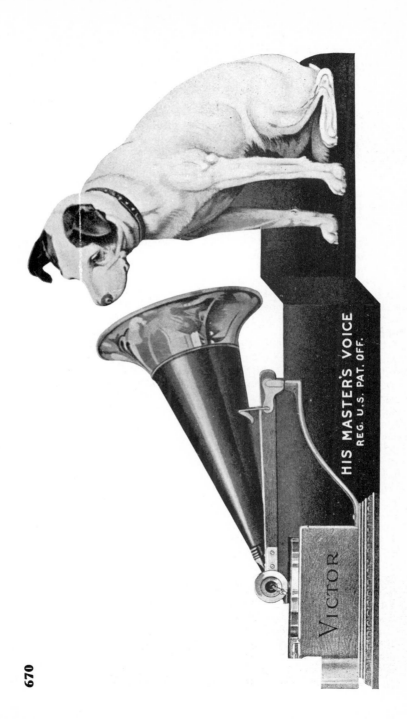

HIS MASTER'S VOICE
REG. U.S. PAT. OFF.

Victor

Ohio, to produce quantities of this 3 foot 5 inch high Dog in papier mache. It weighed approximately 34 lbs when crated for shipment and was sold to Dealers for $10 each (illus no. 671). This continued to be available through 1917 but it seems Wartime conditions then called a temporary halt to its production.

Many Dealers placed these 'giant' 'Nippers' outside the doors of their stores and there are numerous stories of them being attacked and even carried away by the real dogs of the neighbourhood. One of the most amusing was reported from Portland, Oregon on August 5th 1920 when a white battle-scarred Bull Terrier started down Broadway evidently looking for trouble. Opposite the entrance to the Bush & Lane Piano Store he encountered the fixed and immoveable gaze of a three foot papier mache dog which sat all day at the store door. The live dog eyed the papier mache Dog and decided that he didn't like his looks at all. Perhaps the fact that the papier mache Dog paid no attention to him irritated him even further. At any rate the little bull terrier seized the enormous muzzle of the papier mache giant in a deathgrip. The two rolled on the pavement together and a crowd of 200 gathered to witness the struggle. One of the employees of the store dashed through the crush and dragged both the contestants inside the store. Forceable methods had to be applied to separate the terrier from his prey. It was only after the assailant's enthusiasm had been dampened by several gallons of water that the papier mache giant was released and the bull terrier, still breathing defiance, was ejected from the Store.

In February 1919 the Victor Company introduced a smaller Dog, 18 inches high which sold to Dealers for only $1 (illus no. 675). The Company announced: "emerging from a War period when necessary restrictions confronted us, Victor Dealers will welcome this announcement, again making available the famous Victor Dog". The models were offered to Dealers on a clear understanding that it would be used only in the stores of Victor Dealers for display purposes.

In April 1919 a slight variant of the model appeared (illus no. 674) — no price was quoted.

The following month a miniature Victor Dog was produced which measured only 4 inches high overall (illus no. 673). It was manufactured by The Penn Phonograph Company Inc. of Philadelphia.

By July 1919 the 3 foot 5 inch papier mache Dog was back in production selling to Dealers at the old price of $10 each. Both the 18 inch and 3 foot 5 inch Dog continued to be available through 1921 and probably up to 1924.

Meanwhile in Britain the three dimensional Dog was beginning to go out of favour, in fact, the British Company decided in February 1920 that the issue of model Dogs should be discontinued altogether, it being stated "if there was a general desire for advertisements of this character, they should take the form of a cardboard model".

In January 1924 the Victor Company became worried that Dealers were using model Dogs without the companion Gramophone and so decided that the practice of supplying individual papier mache Dogs would be discontinued. In its place the Company issued the 'Victor Trademark Model' (illus no. 676). The Dog and Gramophone was supplied complete, mounted on a substantial base 29 inches long, 12½ inches wide by 1⅞ inches thick. Completely packed it weighed 59 lbs and sold to Dealers at $6 (£1.25). These models were manufactured at a New York Studio where illustration number 678 was taken.

672

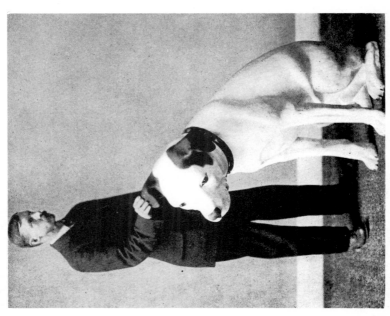

671

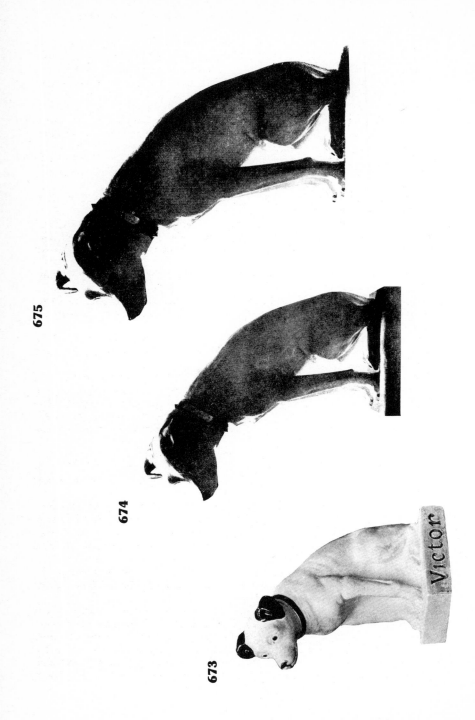

675

674

673

Victor

In February 1925 The Gramophone Company in London made available a similar model (illus no. 677). 750 of these models were ordered by the Company from Models Ltd., Loughborough. These were sold to Dealers at £2 each.

In 1928 The Gramophone Company was, once again, becoming unenthusiastic about the papier mache model 'Nippers' and 'decided to discontinue altogether this particular form of display piece'. We have been unable to establish whether this signalled the end of British manufacture of model 'Nippers' or not. Illustration number 679 shows the British papier mache 'Nipper' and a Trademark Gramophone.

In 1929 the Victor Talking Machine Company became part of the RCA family and the new management continued the use of 'Nipper' on its products, extending his image to radio and later, to television.

In November 1938 a new series of papier mache Dogs was released by RCA — Victor, both large and small sizes being available (illus no. 672).

After the War, in 1947, RCA commissioned the well known sculptor, Carl Hallsthammer, 'to carve an all American model of the original 'Nipper'. The models were produced in two sizes, 11 inch and 36 inch and some 20,000 are said to have been manufactured.

A new series of 'Nippers' for Dealer's use appeared during the 1950's (illus nos 680-681). These are said to have been moulded in rubber.

Also during the 1950's Bronze statues of 'Nipper', mounted on a marble base, were produced. These were awarded to RCA-Victor Distributors and Dealers 'for outstanding achievement'.

During the 1960's a 2 foot high stuffed 'Nipper' toy was offered free in New York City area to every customer who purchased an RCA-Victor black and white portable television set.

In 1965/66 special products division of Tempo Products Company of Cleveland, Ohio, advertised 'Nipper' models in 3 sizes — 10 inch ($14.95), 18 inch ($24.95) and 36 inch (no price given due to special shipping costs). The models were made of high density polyethylene and hand painted. They were advertised as being made available to members of the public for the first time (illus no. 682).

Incredibly the holders of the 'Nipper' Trademark on both sides of the Atlantic began to think of abandoning it during the late 1960's. In both cases 'Nipper' was to be passed over in favour of other Marks for which each Company held the worldwide rights.

E.M.I. planned to go back to its first Trademark 'The Recording Angel' which had been introduced in 1898, but to give it an updated image and to use it together with the letters E.M.I., both of which the Company controlled worldwide, the 'Angel' thus being promoted as their top International Classical Trademark thus virtually eliminating the H.M.V. Dog Label altogether.

Luckily strong opposition from within the Group, particularly from the Overseas Companies saved the day and 'Nipper' still reigns supreme on the EMI Classical recordings.

In 1968 RCA also decided to promote its corporate image in place of the famous 'Nipper'. They even published an 'Introducing a Brand New Record Company' advertisement in which they depicted 'Nipper' and a horn gramophone firmly deposited, with other rubbish, into a waste paper basket! Even worse, just over a year later in April 1969, much to everyone's horror, they removed the famous 'Nipper' stained glass windows from the tower at Camden

676

677

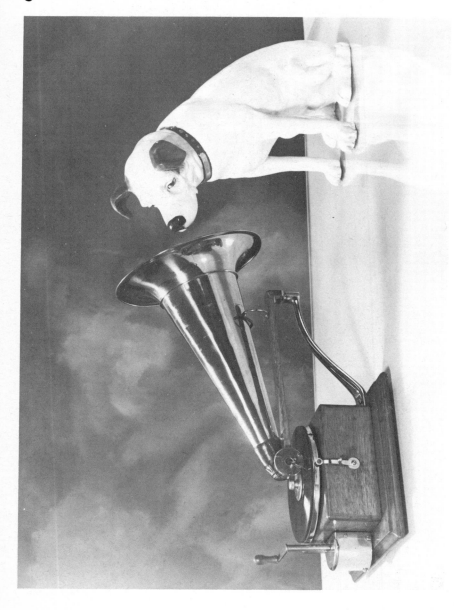

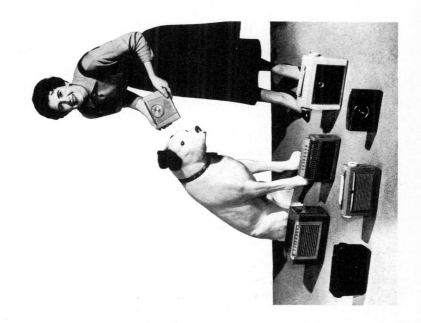

(see reference to this in the 'Buildings' chapter).

For 10 years 'Nipper' was relegated to the second division although he was not entirely forgotten as he still appeared on RCA-Victor record labels in the U.S.A.

When Edgar H. Griffiths became President of RCA in 1976 he began to make long range plans to restore 'Nipper' and the H.M.V. Trademark to a prominent position in the States.

The Old King Cole Company in Louisville, Ohio, recommenced manufacture of the 10 inch, 18 inch and 36 inch 'Nippers', replacing the old papier mache models with a modern plastic variety. Illustration number 683 showing 'Nipper' clones at the Old King Cole Works was issued to coincide with the RCA decision to reinstate 'Nipper' to his old place in his American family.

In 1976 the Antique Phonograph Company of Pasadena, California advertised a 15½ inch high replica of 'Nipper'. They stated that the statue 'was cast from the highest quality oven dried hydrocol plaster'. The blurb goes on 'he is complete in every detail from his cocked head down to his toe nails. He is hand painted and carefully aged to look as if he were stored away in a Dealer's stockroom for fifty years'. The price including shipping was $39.95.

Also on offer was a plaster recreation of the Trademark Gramophone the horn of which was embellished with gold leaf. Illustration number 685 reproduces an advertisement for the hydrocal plaster Dog and Gramophone, whilst illustration number 684 shows an actual set which is in the collection of Diamond 'Jim' Greer of Canada.

Also that year a working reproduction of the 'Trademark' Gramophone was produced in Japan. Once again we are indebted to Diamond 'Jim' Greer for illustration number 686 which shows one of these models in his collection. We have not seen any of these reproductions, however, Allen Koenigsberg reported that they were close copies of the original. Allen also reported that the current serial number in use on these models was J 18425 on the reproducer and 34431 on the motor housing. The price for these reproductions in the U.S.A. was $425. As far as we know they were not generally available in the U.K. No special model of 'Nipper' was produced for this unit.

In November of the same year Easton Musical Antiques of West Orange, New Jersey advertised 'fully authorised "Nippers" from the original RCA mould' — 10 inch ($29.95), 18 inch ($49.95) and 36 inch ($89.95) (illus no. 688). These were produced in a polyethylene material. The style of this advertisement was similar to the earlier one by the Tempo Products Company.

The following year Oliver Berliner (Grandson of Emile Berliner) offered a 'unique replica' of the famous Dog and Gramophone. This was an electric version which played the modern 7 inch 45 rpm discs which were reproduced through a speaker set into the brass horn. The Gramophone came complete with a 16 inch high 'Nipper', produced in polyethylene and was hand painted. Only 100 of these units are said to have been produced, they came complete with a 7 inch recording of the voice of Emile Berliner and a booklet describing the history of the 'His Master's Voice' Trademark and the inventions of Emile Berliner.

The units were produced as part of the celebrations of the hundredth anniversary of the first reproduction of recorded sound. They were available from The Berliner Gramophone Company of California, price complete $595.00. Diamond 'Jim' Greer of Canada, has one of these Oliver Berliner models, this is

682

Now Available in Limited Quantities

Famous "NIPPER"* Dog Symbol

Unusual gift - Collectors item - Conversation piece

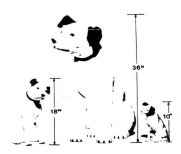

"Nipper,"* the famed dog, a symbol of RCA's "His Master's Voice" advertising programs, continues to win friends. Life-like, hand painted, sturdy, high density polyethylene models of the concentrating canine are available in limited quantities to the general public for the first time. This unusual conversation piece is available in three sizes, 10", 18" and 36" in height. They are a natural for memorabilia collectors, and make unusual premiums. For those who have almost everything, a little "Nipper" might be the fun answer you've been looking for.

*Trademark used with permission and under license from trademark owner, RCA Corporation.

For additional information write:

TEMPO PRODUCTS COMPANY
AN ALCO STANDARD COMPANY
6200 Cochran Road / Cleveland, Ohio 44139 U.S.A.

ALCO
The Corporate Partnership

J 6-1M

685

"BERLINER" and "NIPPER"

"His Master's Voice" trademark is owned by RCA Corp. Now for the first time you can own a complete *Trademark* display! Both the "Berliner" and "Nipper" replicas shown are cast from the highest quality, oven-dried, hydrocal plaster (not styrofoam). They are hand-painted and carefully aged to look like they were stored away for over 50 years. The horn on the "Berliner" is gold-leafed and the other metal parts are silver-leafed. "Nipper is nicely detailed right down to his toenails. He stands 14½" high.

"BERLINER" only $49.95
"NIPPER" only $39.95

All orders shipped prepaid and insured within U.S. (Calif. residents, please add 6% sales tax). Complete satisfaction or return for full refund. Send check or money order in full payment to:

ANTIQUE PHONOGRAPH COMPANY
35 East St. Joseph Street
Dept. M
Arcadia, Calif. 91006

686

687

shown in illustration number 687.

'Nipper' models have appeared in other sizes, smaller and larger than the ones described above.

In 1954, Pytron Ltd. of New Malden Surrey, constructed two giant models of 'Nipper' and his famous Gramophone (illus nos. 689-690). It was intended that one of these should dominate the H.M.V. Stand (No. 10) at the Northern Radio Show at Manchester. One model still exists and is proudly displayed over the main doorway of the EMI Records Production and Distribution Building, Uxbridge Road, Hayes.

Rumour has it that the second model was actually stolen from one of the Radio Show display stands and the Company never saw it again. However Mr L.G. Wood who later became Main Board Group Director, Records, cannot recall the incident. Collectors casting an envious eye on the remaining model be warned — the Company also treasures it!

An even larger 'Nipper' — the world's largest in fact — is 25½ feet high and weighs 4 tons. He sits on top of the Headquarters Building of the RTA, an RCA Distributor in Albany, New York. He was hoisted up their in 1954 and has remained in place ever since.

He was built by a Chicago Design Firm who covered his complex steel skeleton with a special weather resistant composition. The cost of the Dog with special steel platform and his raising into place produced a bill for $8,000. The highest portion of this huge statue is the Dog's right ear which now includes a flashing beacon in it to alert any low flying aircraft in the vicinity.

The RCA Press Release of the Dog states "during his 34 years as an unofficial mascot of Albany, 'Nipper' has weathered many rain, sleet and snow storms as well as winds up to 70 miles an hour . . . Today the Dog's main admirers fall into three categories: tourists, pigeons and painters. Out of town visitors driving near the RTA building frequently change their travel plans to let children see a good close up of the giant pooch". He gets repainted every three to five years (illus no. 691) and looks all set for a further thirty years looking out over Albany.

In recent years, starting in the 1950's, a whole series of small 'Nippers' have been produced in china and plastic. They have appeared as statues, money boxes or banks and even as salt and pepper shakers.

In 1952 NV Nederlansche Gramofon Maatschappij of Holland produced a porcelain finished Dog and Gramophone as a Salt and Pepper Set (illus no. 692). These sets were issued by the Company as Christmas gifts to their customers in 1952. Other examples of 'Nipper' Salt and Pepper Sets appear in illustration numbers 697-699.

Illustration number 693 shows a cream coloured plastic Nipper 'Boxer' Dog adopting a pugilistic stand. It would seem that the model was following the reputation of the original 'Nipper' who was known to enjoy a good scrap with another dog when he got the chance. The model stands 15 inches high on an oval shaped base. The back of the collar bears the words 'RCA Victor'. We do not know the history of this piece which would appear to date from the 1960's.

A small 'Nipper' 3 inches tall produced in highly glazed ceramic with hand painted features was sold complete with a metal pencil sharpener Gramophone by 'The Lighter Side' Mt. Clemens, Michigan for $6.98 in 1983 (illus no. 695).

A piece of British seaside pottery from Dymchurch shows a rather pathetic puppy, with a patch over one eye, listening to the Gramophone. Perhaps he's just heard one of the rival companies' records. The words 'His Master's Voice'

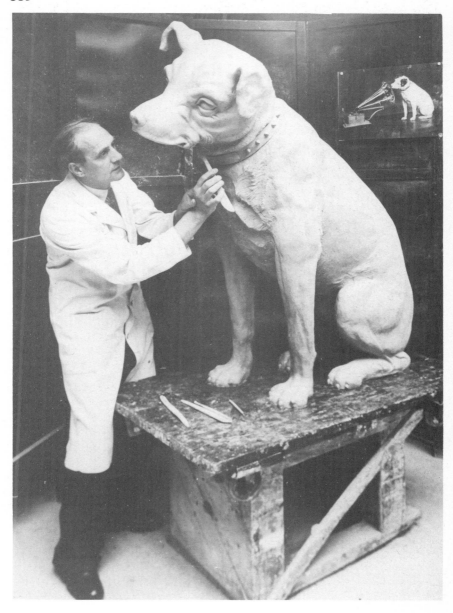

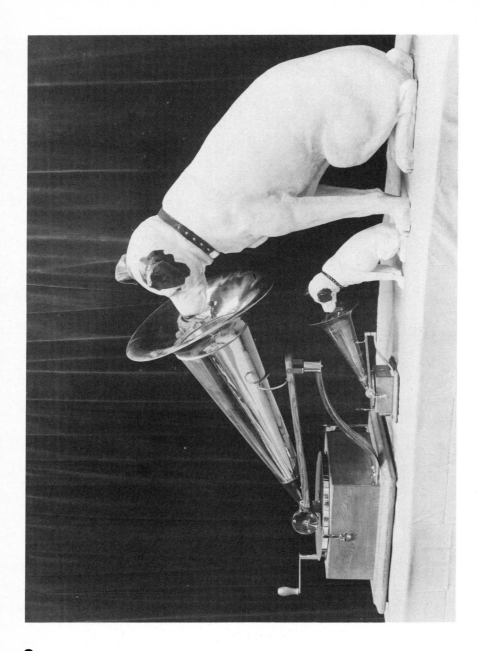

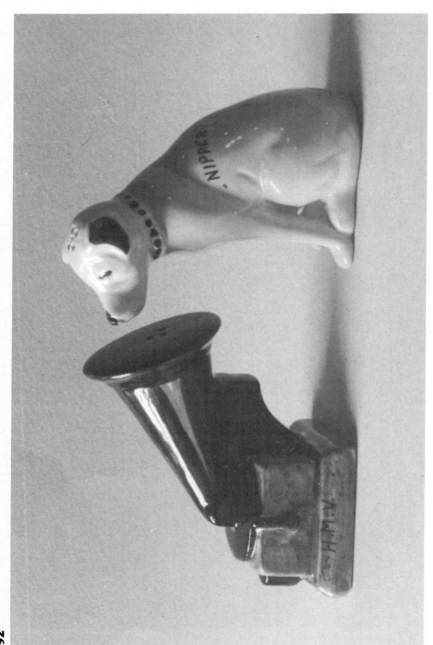

written on a stave over musical notes appears round the back (illus no. 700).

Sarsaparilla of New York have marketed a fine series of five ceramic 'Nipper's' — 2½ inch, 3 inch, 6½ inch, 9 inch and 12 inches high. The two largest are money boxes, the three smaller being purely statues (illus no. 701).

During 1977 Gerry Oord, then Managing Director of EMI Records in London, gave to a select and privileged few a china 'Nipper' and china Gramophone, both modelled in Italy (illus no. 702). It was said, at the time, that they had been specially modelled for Mr Oord; they are certainly desirable collectors items.

In 1970 the Tokio Idea Centre manufactured a Crystal Nipper in pale blue glass (illus no. 694). This is very attractive and stands 7 inches high. It sold in Japan for Yen 1,800.

In 1983 'Downes Collectors Showcase' of Milwaukee advertised 'the Nipper bank in glazed porcelain with padded paws for table top protection' (Illus no. 696). The 9 inch model cost $24.95 and the 6 inch high Dog $14.95.

Various other china 'Nipper' banks have been seen. These were either unmarked or shown to be of Japanese origin.

Although in Britain during 1981/84 various 'Nipper Dog Offers' were made in the National Press, all supplies of the model Dog appear to have come from one source — Leroco Exports Ltd. of Bourne Road, Bexley, Kent. The models were made in Japan. Leroco Exports who are the sole agents tell us that over 10,000 china 'Nippers' have been sold by them during the past three years. Illustration number 703 shows one of the special promotional adverts — it appeared in the Daily Star in July 1982.

Some very special 'Nipper' statues must also be mentioned here. Allen Koenigsberg in his Antique Phonograph Monthly Magazine for November 1973 drew the attention of collectors to a remarkable 'life sized Nipper' made in solid 24 carat gold (illus no. 705).

This remarkable statue was made by Tiffany and Co. of America for exhibition on the Victor Talking Machine Company's Stand at the St. Louis Exposition in 1904. As Allen remarks "Victor strongly implied here that the work was already completed and on display at the Victor exhibit, but what lucky collector (or banker) has seen a 24 carat Nipper'.

On February 8th 1978 a small solid silver 'Nipper' and Gramophone on an ebonised plinth came up for sale at Christies, South Kensington. This carried the Birmingham Hallmark of 1935 and appeared to have been presented to an S.E. Chalk (illus no. 704). It weighed 3¾ ounces gross and was on a fitted casket. It was sold at the auction for £520. Before the sale, EMI Music Archives were consulted but were unable to produce any information on the source of this model. It is not known whether this was one of a series made for presentation during King George V's Silver Jubilee Year or whether it was a unique item.

A very modern 'Nipper' is to be found in the entrance hall of the RCA Space Mountain at Disney World in Florida. The Dog and his Gramophone encased in their space capsule seem set to conquer brave new worlds, however distant they may be.

694

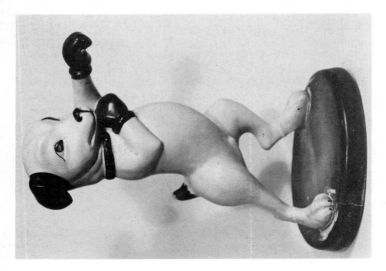

693

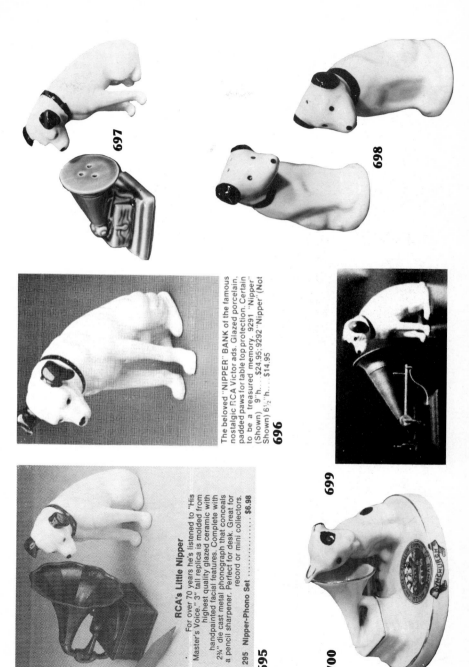

697

698

The beloved "NIPPER" BANK of the famous nostalgic RCA Victor ads. Glazed porcelain, padded paws for table top protection. Certain to be a treasured memory. 9291 "Nipper" (Shown) 9" h.....$24.95; 9292 "Nipper" (Not Shown) 6½" h.....$14.95

696

699

RCA's Little Nipper

For over 70 years he's listened to "His Master's Voice." 3" tall replica is molded from highest quality glazed ceramic with handpainted facial features. Complete with 2¾" die cast metal phonograph that conceals a pencil sharpener. Perfect for desk. Great for record or mini collectors.

295 **Nipper-Phono Set** **$6.98**

695

700

S.E.CHALK.

Postlude

Years ago the question was asked "Did Caruso make the Gramophone or, did the Gramophone make Caruso?" Coming to the end of this digest containing illustrations of over 700 items and descriptions of even more, one is tempted to ask "where would the Gramophone and Victor Companies be without Nipper?" Certainly the two Gramophones appearing on the opposite page are feeling somewhat lost without the little Dog sitting there listening to them.

The record label in illustration number 706 dates from 1920. When the now independent Deutsche Grammophon Actiengesellschaft wished to export its records it found that it was not entitled to use the 'His Master's Voice' Trademark outside the borders of Germany; they therefore discretely lost 'Nipper' the Dog and added the inscription 'Musica G.D.'

The Gramophone in illustration number 707 was made in Singapore by 'Tomy'. He too is frantically looking for a 'Nipper' to listen to him. Wind him up and he dashes around waving his hands, shaking his horn and violently playing his record. It all goes to prove that a Talking Machine is really not quite a 'Gramophone' without his little Dog.

But what of 'Nipper' himself, how does he feel sitting on his famous record label endlessly listening to his very long playing gramophone? An indignant Danish lady wrote to the magazine 'Copenhagen'. In her letter she noted "I protest against the Dog on 'His Master's Voice' records going backwards. The Dog must be dizzy — and to what purpose? I am getting a complex from it. The outcome is that I cannot play my beautiful records until the Dog goes round the other way!"

Now, what, we ask ourselves, does 'Nipper' think about it all?

706

"GRAMOPHONE=RECORD"

Abendlied
von Robert Schumann
...re Dux, Kammersängerin

Katalog No
043353

Bestell No
76407

707

A 'Nipper' Chronology'

together with some brief information which may be of help to the reader.

	1884	A black and white fox terrier was born in Bristol. He was called 'Nipper' by the family who was to own him (due to his tendency to nip the back of people's legs).
		Two persons present when Nipper was first brought to his new home in Bristol as a 3 month old puppy by their father, Mark Henry Barraud, stated that this occurred in 1884.
September	1895	After he had suffered a stroke at the age of 11, Nipper became paralysed in his hind quarters. He was buried under a mulberry tree in Durham's Gardens (77 Clarence Street), Kingston-upon-Thames.
	c.1898	It is not known exactly when Francis Barraud painted the first version of the picture 'His Master's Voice'. In a sworn statement dated January 12th 1921 he declared "the said painting was entirely my own original work ... It was originally designed and painted by me *sometime prior to the year 1899* but in its original form the dog was listening to a phonograph which was a cylinder machine".
April	1898	The Gramophone Company is formed by Trevor Williams and Barry Owen. At this time it is a small Private Trading Syndicate with £15,000 credit.
	1899	'E. Berliner', Montreal, is formed by J. Sanders and E. Blount.
February 11	1899	Francis Barraud filed an application for 'Memorandum of Assignment of Copyright' of his picture of 'Dog Looking At and Listening To A Phonograph'.
May 31	1899	This is the date it is thought that Francis Barraud called at The Gramophone Company's Office in Maiden Lane where he left a photograph of his painting of the Dog listening to a phonograph.
June 2	1899	Barry Owen, the General Manager of The Gramophone Company, wrote to Barraud asking him to call on him either on the morning of Saturday June 3rd or during Monday June 5th.
June	1899	During this month negotiations took place between Barraud and The Gramophone Company on a purchase price for the picture.
August 25	1899	The Gramophone Company Limited is formed in London.
September 15	1899	The Gramophone Company sent a letter to Barraud

making a formal offer for the picture. The purchase of the Painting was conditional on Barraud painting out the Phonograph and repainting it with the then current model of the Gramophone.

September 16	1899	Barraud accepted the offer by telegram.
October 4	1899	Representatives of The Gramophone Company called at Barraud's studio, 126 Piccadilly, London at 3 o'clock to view the altered picture.
October 12	1899	Barraud sent the Company the first photograph to be taken of the revised picture.
October 17	1899	The actual painting was delivered to the offices of The Gramophone Company Ltd.
October 18	1899	Barraud acknowledged receipt of a first payment of £50 from the Company which gave to the Company sole reproduction rights of the picture.
December 5	1899	Proofs of the first reproduction of the painting (printed by Rembrandt & Intagalis Ptg. Co of Lancaster) were available.
December 12	1899	Perfect copies of the reproduction were printed.
end December	1899	Copies of reproduction available to the Trade.
January	1900	The 'His Master's Voice' pictures makes its first appearance on the British Record Supplement for the month.
January 29	1900	The Company pays Barraud a further £50 for the transfer of the Copyright of the 'His Master's Voice' picture to the Company, making a total purchase price of £100 paid to Barraud.
February 5	1900	The Gramophone Company applied for 'Memorandum of the Assignment of Copyright of the Painting of Dog Looking Into and Listening To A Gramophone and entitled "His Master's Voice".'
March 6	1900	Barraud wrote to Barry Owen that he had painted a small watercolour of 'His Master's Voice' about 12 inches by 10 inches which he wished to exhibit. It was shown at the Royal Institute of Painters and Watercolourists where it was sold for 15 guineas.
April 1	1900	Barraud agreed to make a further copy in exactly the same style as the watercolour shown at the Exhibition. This was for Barry Own who purchased the copy for 15 guineas. It was delivered to Owen during June 1900. The *original* watercolour was traced and eventually purchased by The Gramophone Company in June 1956. The copy presumably went to America with Barry Owen when he left the Company.
April-May	1900	Emile Berliner came to Britain for negotiations with Trevor Lloyd Williams (Chairman of The Gramophone Company Ltd.). During this time he is thought to have seen the original 'His Master's Voice' painting.
May	1900	On his return to America Berliner called Barry Owen requesting 'Will you assign me copyright Master's Voice

for America, cable answer", on which Barry Owen has written "Yes, writing W.B.O.". Berliner began to use the picture from this day.

May 26	1900	Berliner applied to Register the 'His Master's Voice' picture as a Trademark. The picture he submitted was a carefully drawn pen sketch of the Dog and machine about 4½ inches wide by 3½ inches deep. His required statement dated May 26 1900 said "My Trademark consists of the picture of a dog in the act of listening to the sound issuing from the horn of a machine. Underneath the said picture appear the words 'His Master's Voice' — but this is unimportant and may be omitted since the essential feature of the Trademark is the picture of the dog listening to the sound reproducing machine. This Trademark I have used continuously in my business since May 24th 1900".
May 28	1900	Berliner applied to the Canadian Minister of Agriculture (Trade Mark & Copyright Branch) for Registration of the 'His Master's Voice' Trade Mark. He also applied for Canadian Registration of the copyright of the picture of "Dog listening to a Talking Machine".
June 6	1900	Canadian Trade Mark (7366) and Copyright Registration (11433) is granted to Emile Berliner.
June 10	1900	The U.S. Patent Office issued a "Trade Mark for Gramophones" (34890) to Emile Berliner.
September/ October	1900	The 'His Master's Voice' Trademark appears on the backs of new Berliner records in Canada.
September	1900	E.R. Johnson starts to trade as 'The Consolidated Talking Machine Company' in America and to use the 'Dog' Trademark.
December	1900	E.R. Johnson begins to use the Trademark 'Victor' in the U.S.A.
December 10	1900	The Gramophone Company Ltd. transfers its business to a newly incorporated Company, Registered as The Gramophone & Typewriter Limited.
December 22	1900	The British Gramophone Company by now having changed its name to The Gramophone & Typewriter Ltd. applied for Registration of the 'His Master's Voice' picture (without words) as a Trademark.
March 19	1901	The British Patents Office advised The British Company of the Registration of the 'His Master's Voice' picture as a Trademark (No. 235053).
October 3	1901	E.R. Johnson formed the Victor Talking Machine Company which was incorporated on this day. The Company contined to use the 'His Master's Voice' picture together with the word 'Victor' as its Trademarks.
	1901	The Victor Talking Machine Company assumed the American Rights for the 'His Master's Voice' painting and adopted it as its Trademark.

December	1903	Nipper appears on British Gramophone Company needle boxes.
	1904	The Gramophone Company cedes the Exclusive Rights to Gramophone Sales to the Territory of Japan to the Victor Talking Machine Company, who now hold the Rights to use the 'Dog' Trademark in Japan.
April 8	1904	'E. Berliner' Montreal, now becomes The Berliner Gramophone Company of Canada Ltd.
March 5	1906	The American 'Rights' in the 'His Master's Voice' Trademark *officially* transferred from Berliner to the Victor Talking Machine Company.
November 18	1907	The title of The Gramophone & Typewriter Limited now reverts back to The Gramophone Company Limited.
	1908	Victor introduce Double-sided Black Label Records.
February	1909	Nipper appears on British Record Labels for the first time — on records issued on the February Supplementary List from London.
June 17	1909	The Berliner Gramophone Company of Canada becomes a Limited Company. Victor Talking Machine Company hold some of its shares.
July	1909	Nipper appears on the British Company's Gramophone Instrument Catalogue.
July 22	1910	The Gramophone Company applied to Register the 'His Master's Voice' picture together with the words 'His Master's Voice' as a Trademark.
November	1910	This Registration (No. 325592) was notified by the British Patent Office.
October	1910	The Gramophone Company applied for Registration of 'His Master's Voice' (the words only).
January	1911	This Registration (No. 327785) was notified by the British Patent Office.
December	1910	The 'Dog' Mark together with the words 'His Master's Voice' now replaced the word 'Gramophone' on all the products of the British Company.
late	1911	The famous 'Nipper' weather vane, designed by Mr Blomfield, is installed on top of the Clock Tower of The Gramophone Company's Head Office at Hayes in Middlesex.
August	1912	The Gramophone Company issued its first 'His Master's Voice' double-sided records on a newly introduced Plum Label.
April 17	1913	By this date Francis Barraud had 'laid in the replica' of the first copy he was to make of his 'His Master's Voice' painting.
April 22	1913	The finished painting is handed to The Gramophone Company for onward transmission to the Victor Talking Machine company. This was the copy made for E.R. Johnson.
May 29	1913	Francis Barraud accepts a commission from The Gramophone Company to 'varnish and renovate' the

		original 'His Master's Voice' painting. He was paid £5/15/0 for this.
October	1914	The Gramophone Company issued its famous 'Dreadnought' poster taken from an original painting by Francis Barraud.
	1915	Four stained glass windows of 'Nipper', each measuring 14½ feet in diameter, designed by Nicola D'Ascenzo were installed in the tower of the Cabinet Factory of the Victor Talking Machine Company at Camden, New Jersey, U.S.A.
	1917	The Bystander published a cartoon drawn by Francis Barraud, showing the head of a pugnatious British Bulldog emerging from the gramophone horn and frightening away the spiked helmeted dachshund.
December 5	1919	The Victor Company joins with The Gramophone Company in granting Francis Barraud an annuity of £250 a year, to start from January 1st 1920.
	1920	The Victor Company purchases 51% interest in The Gramophone Company of London and so gains control.
	1921	Oil paint reproductions of the 'His Master's Voice' painting offered by the Victor Company.
July 20	1921	The Gramophone Company's new store in Oxford Street, London, is opened by Sir Edward Elgar. At this time it is exclusively dedicated to 'Nipper' and 'Nipper' Brand products.
	1923	The Victor Company issued Double-sided Red Seal Records.
November 21	1923	The Victor Talking Machine Company purchase control of the Berliner Gramophone Company of Canada and its subsidiary and the name of the Company is changed to The Victor Talking Machine Company of Canada Ltd.
	1924	Francis Barraud hand paints the 'His Master's Voice' Trademark on the miniature gramophone placed into Queen Mary's Dolls House.
March 14	1924	The joint annuity to Francis Barraud is increased to £350 from March 31st 1924.
April	1924	The Gramophone Company issued double-sided Red Label 'His Master's Voice' Celebrity Records.
August 29	1924	Francis Barraud dies, in his 68th year, at his house in St. John's Wood, London.
December	1924	It was stated that the total spent, to date, on advertising the 'Dog' was £5,000,000.
January 6	1927	E.R. Johnson sells out control of the Victor Talking Machine Company to a Banking Syndicate — Speyer & Co. and J.W. Seligmann of New York.
	1927	Victor Talking Machine Company of Japan Ltd. formed.
	1928	Victor sold 32% interest in the Victor Talking Machine Company of Japan Ltd.
	1928	Victor gain full ownership of the Canadian Company.
March 15	1929	RCA gains control of the Victor Talking Machine Company.

April 21	1931	The Gramophone Company Limited and the Columbia Graphophone Company Limited join to form Electric and Musical Industries Ltd (E.M.I.).
	1934	The Victor Talking Machine Company of Canada changes its title to RCA Victor Company Limited.
December 26	1937	The H.M.V. Store in Oxford Street is partially destroyed by fire.
May 8	1939	The H.M.V. Store in Oxford Street reopens after the fire of December 1937.
	1950	To mark the 50th anniversary of the formation of the Australian Company the original 'His Master's Voice' painting was sent to Australia for exhibition.
August 4	1950	E.M.I. sponsored an attempt to find and exhume 'Nipper's' bones from the site of his burial at Kingston-upon-Thames.
March	1951	The original 'His Master's Voice' painting is reframed and placed into a genuine Louis XVth frame.
August-September	1951	The 'His Master's Voice' painting is placed on display in the exhibition of 'Ten Decades of British Taste' which was held in London and York.
June 29	1952	The original 'His Master's Voice' painting goes to the U.S.A. where it went on exhibition as part of the launching celebrations of 'His Master's Voice' Long Playing Records in America.
	1954	The world's largest 'Nipper' is hoisted into place onto the roof of 911 Broadway, Albany. The 'Dog' is 25½ feet high and weighs four tons.
	1954	A giant 'Nipper' and Gramophone is displayed by The Gramophone Company on its stand at the Earl's Court Radio Show. The Dog is 4 feet 6 inches high whilst the Gramophone's turntable is 21 inches in diameter and the brass horn 4 feet 3 inches long and 2 feet 9 inches across the mouth.
November 25	1960	'Nipper' appears on the Coat of Arms of Sir Joseph Lockwood, then Chairman of E.M.I.
January 1	1971	Electric & Musical Industries Ltd (E.M.I. Ltd) changes its name to EMI Ltd. This was done for two reasons "first because our present name no longer reflects our wide span of activities and interests, secondly, the initials 'EMI' have become our primary means of identification throught the world."
November 28	1973	To mark the seventy-fifth anniversary of The Gramophone Company, Ind Coope remodelled and renamed the old 'Marlborough Head' public house in Great Marlborough Street, to re-open it as 'the Dog and Trumpet', dedicated to Nipper, the H.M.V. Dog.
September	1984	HMV Record Shops organize the unveiling of a plaque to commemorate Nipper's final resting place at 77 Clarence Street, Kingston, Surrey — now a branch of Lloyds Bank.

Acknowledgements

'Nipper' writes to thank all those persons and organizations who have given their time to assist in the construction of this book about him, especially.

The Record Companies of:

RCA (U.S.A. and Canada)

JVC (Japan)

EMI (Britain, Europe & International)

All of whom have allowed illustrations of their souvenir and advertising products to be reproduced in this volume.

Messrs Harrison's Ltd., the Printers

who have permitted the reproduction of a photograph from their House Magazine 'Informe'

Christie's (South Kensington) Ltd

who granted permission for use of the photograph from

Jan-Feb 1978 Sales Catalogue

Allen Koenigsberg

who has granted permission for reproduction of material which appeared in his publication 'Antique Phonograph Monthly'

Mr Venables of Leroco Exports Ltd.

for information on the sales of their ceramic models of 'Nipper'

Mrs Ruth Lambert, Messrs Frank Andrews, George Frow, Diamond 'Jim' Greer, Victor Lanza and Leonard G. Wood

all of whom have kindly loaned valuable 'Nipper' souvenirs from their collections for photographing.

Last, but certainly not least, 'Nipper' thanks all the following persons who have helped along this project:

Robbin Ahrold *Divisional Vice-President Communications RCA*
Philip Barraud *The Great-Nephew of Francis Barraud, the artist*
George Brock-Nannestad *A Danish Collector and Patent Expert*
Peter Buckleigh *Managing Director EMI Music International Services Ltd., Japan*
Douglas Coates *Marketing Manager, HMV Shops Ltd.*
Mort Gaffin *Director Corporate Identification & Exhibits RCA*
Ian Gray *Managing Director HMV Shops Ltd.*
William Green *Artist, now retired from Messrs Harrisons Ltd., the Printers*
Nicholas Hampton *Managing Director EMI Australia Ltd*
Wilfried Jung *EMI Regional Director Central Europe*
Hanne Kristensen *Managing Director EMI Dansk-Engelsk A/S*
Roel Kruize *Managing Director EMI Holland*
Tony Locantro *Manager Royalty Administration and Licensing, ICD*
Sir Joseph Lockwood *Chairman of EMI 1954-1974*
Francois Minchin *Former EMI Regional Director, Southern Europe*
Peter Morgan *Photographer*
Gerlinde Platford *Production Documentation Officer, ICD*
Trevor Rawd *Ex employee of C.R. Spouge, Lincoln*
Alexis Rotelli *Managing Director EMI Italiana SpA*
John Wolfson *Collector and Record Historian in the U.S.A.*
L.G. Wood, C.B.E. *Former EMI Main Board and Group Director, Records*

The illustration at the top of the previous page comes from EMI's Magazine 'Music Talk'.